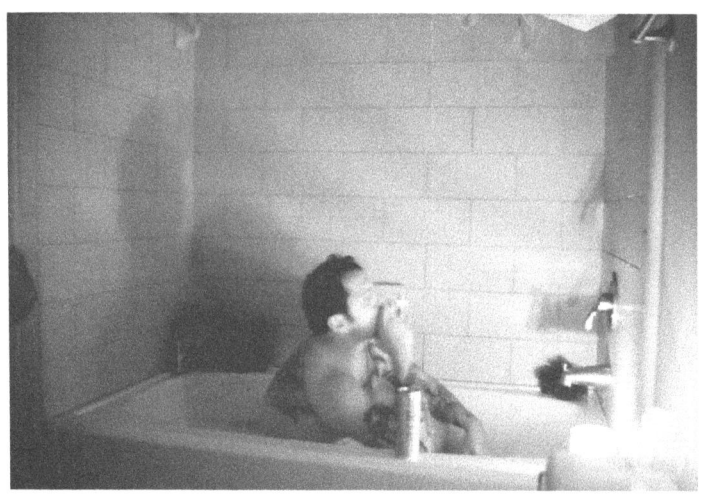

Demons in the Taillights

William Bolyard

Copyright © 2024 William Bolyard
First Edition | First Printing

All rights reserved.
This book or any portion thereof
May not be used or reproduced in any fashion whatsoever
Without the permission of the publisher or the author
Except for the use of quotations

Publisher: Dead Reckoning Collective
Book Cover Design: Tyler James Carroll
Book Cover Photo: William Bolyard
Editor: Keith Walter Dow

Printed in the United States of America

Library of Congress Control Number: 2024936771

ISBN-13: 978-1-963803-03-7 (paperback)

This is for all my lovers and friends.
Thanks for keeping me around.

Mortality	16
Close It Up	17
Fuck, Why Am I Here?	18
Trailers And Corn	19
Untitled No. 4	20
The Naked Bunch	21
Prairies And Prayers	22
Pool	24
Shit, What Time Is It?	26
Do You Accept The Charges?	27
French Jazz	28
Dear Future Wife,	29
Nude Therapy	30
I Hate Myself	32
Not Me	34
Dr. Suess	35
W Henry Street	36
HWY 96	37
Just Another Politician	38
From The Note	39
Burnout Underground	40
Un-Published And Unkept	41
Here We Are Again	42
It's All Kind Of Dumb	43
Wildflowers By The Highway	44
HWY 20	45
Pub On Fire	46
Demon In The Taillights	47
Dive	48
Cobblestone	49
Saure Kommt Heute	50
A Modern Howl	51
Suicide Note	52
Book Talk	53
Frostbite	54
Honestly	55
Ceiling Fires	56
Red Bananas	57
War Bad, Make Me Sad	58
Afghan Scarf	60
HWY 11	61
The Road House	62
Squatters	63
Old Town	64
Forgotten Cards	65
Fuck, Your Eyes Are Beautiful	66
There It Ws	67
Seven Years	68
Dream Journal #531	69
Hyde	70
Chefs, Writers & Painters	71
Worn Out Blues	72
Van Life	74
Dream Journal #27	76
Border Towns	77
Always Another Round	78
End Of An Era	79
A Cold Day In Hell	80
Why Can't We?	81
Short Dreams	82
12 Grams	84
Okay, But Why?	86
No Need To Rush	87
Beat Up Toney Lamas	88
Stew	90
Horror	91
Reset	92
Soundtrack To The Night	93
Back On The Grind	94
Going Through [...]	95
Another Round	96
Went West	98
Foreign Porch	100
Groceries	101
Danced To Death	102
Low-Lit Street Lights	103
Ashtray	104
Heartache Road	105
Short Stories	106
Beach Release	107
Lies	108
Close Out	109
Depressed And Undressed	110
What Is 'It?'	112
That Makes It All Worth Living	114

Title	Page
10 PM on a Tuesday	115
Driving Lighting	116
Black Cadillac	118
Rock Bottom Again	119
Not So Inclined	120
Late Fucking Nights	122
Scotch	123
Superstitions	124
Abstract	126
Tattoos	128
Payphone	129
Cash in the Good Book	130
Good Times	131
Words	132
Cocaine and Tears	134
Paris	135
Oklahoma [...]	136
Camden	137
Lazy J.	138
The One I Didn't Plan	139
Fireflies	140
Gin and Eggs	141
Office	142
Calling the Kettle Black	144
C.C. Me in That	145
Cold Nuggets	146
Red Well	148
Mood Right?	149
Fires	150
Lucy	151
Rupi Kaur and other Micro-Poets	152
Expansion	154
Talks with Patty	155
Too Damn Young	156
The Weight of Love	158
Packed Cars	160
I Thought It Was Clever With Time	162 163
Reds	164
The Law of [...]	165
Silence the World	166
4/5	167
Lame	168
Oil Slick	170
Thursday 9:45	171
Golden Tubs	172
Infant of Prague	173
Land Before he Sea	174
God's a Cunt	175
Orange Piano	176
Roadside Rope Swing	177
That One [...]	178
Feelings	180
Napkin	181
Sobriety	182
Talking to my Demons	183
Prompt Too	184
Evelyn	186
The Last Heartbreak	187
Drinking with Ghosts	188
Drunk & Happy	189
January 15th	190
Stetson Surfer	191
Bad Habits	192
Gutters	194
Hotel Backyard	195
Marshians	196
On the Counter Again	197
This Time	198
Grape	199
Poetry Contest [...]	200
RGV	201
Future	202
Border Madness	203
Woodland	204
Trazodone	206
Fake Tropics	208
741	209
Red Fire	210
Aging	212
Tuesday, 12 PM	213
Dreams	214
Payphone Blues	215
Le Cafe	216
Molecule of Madness	218

BOARDING CALL	220
SOBER	221
TRAVEL	222
HOUSE	224
I HOPE YOU HATE IT	225
THE ROAD	226
ANIMALS IN THE CLOUDS	227
SIMPLE WAS DEATH	228
90'S COUNTRY SONG	229
A CITY I SHOULDN'T LOVE	230
GUESS I'LL WRITE	231
MY SMALL DESERT FRIEND	232
WILMINGTON	234
LAST PAGE	235

Out on the road today, I saw a Sub Pop sticker on a Subaru
A little voice inside my head said, "Yuppies smell teen spirit too."
I thought I knew what love was, but I was blind
Those days are gone forever, whatever, never mind.

Rob Sheffield, Love is a Mix Tape

How we got here:

The summer I wrote this book, I spent a lot of time lying on the floor listening to records. I'd watch my fan spin round and round for hours, only stopping to change one vinyl to another and maybe to grab another beer. I didn't even want to write a book this time. I was trying to figure some shit out, just like we all have been for the last couple of years. Sometimes I feel crazy thinking it all has to be wrong. The psychedelics along the way didn't help as much as I thought they would, but I did have a good time. Still, I had this cold, empty feeling that is so hard to run from. How is it that in the most connected world humanity has ever resided in, people feel less and less? Maybe I'm just turning into a cynic. I thought that a lot. So I went to therapy. Part of me went as an experiment of modern mental health treatment. The other was to find out if I was, in fact, completely crazy. Sadly, it turns out I was not crazy. After a full year with the shrink, she revealed to me that I was, in fact, "Just feeling the same as every other late twenty-year-old..." What a bummer. After that, a book seemed like a pretty good idea.

MORTALITY

I laid on the floor,
Old books
Were strung beside my body.
The words danced in melancholy
Across my brain
Giving up all things holy.
Long ago,
I stared at the ceiling
And drifted,
Just trying to find a reason to stay.

Close It Up

People ask,
"Why do you drink so much?"
Well, it's pretty damn fun.
Up late in my home
Reading old books
Listening to new music
Writing down my thoughts.
Like these:
Sobriety is the biggest form of discipline one can keep.
I respect all that take it on,
I'm weak.
It's so much easier to exist behind the fog.
It could be worse though,
I could be religious.

Fuck, Why Am I Here?

Last night I almost ended it again.
I always come close,
But then I wake up
Alone on the floor.
Hungover from the source.
The booze saves me,
Yet also causes my problem.
Not always,
Mostly it's loneliness.
The emptiness of my soul,
Lost without self-control.
Fuck,
Why am I here?
Guess I'll have another.
Hopefully it will knock me out.
To save me from myself.

Trailers and Corn

I'm from a dying place,
Where everything's old, and people never leave.
There is no industry here.
Just farming,
Trailers and corn.
Maybe some cannabis in the season.

Untitled No. 4

I'm drunk.
Lying in bed,
Trying to remember what I just said.
I'll probably have to leave soon,
Because the windows smell of June.
I'm tired
Of lying with the dead,
Trying to remember what they said.
They left way too soon,
Because life smells like a heroine spoon.
I'm lying in bed,
Drunk,
Naked,
Almost as if I'm awake.
Fighting with the snake inside my brain,
That put simply, is driving me insane.
I'm lying in bed,
Drunk,
Naked,
And bleeding.
From the pain that's in my mind.
That's constantly re-sealing old wounds,
Just to open them again.
As a hobby.
In a copy
Of some abandoned hotel lobby,
Where the phone rings nonstop
And no one answers.
Because we are the cancer.

I'm drunk,
Lying in bed,
Trying to remember all the words I forgot I said,
Just wishing she wasn't dead.

The Naked Brunch

Sunday evening,
I dropped my smokes in the tub.
I was able to save the gin,
But the luckies were a huge loss.
Smoking in a hot bath is close to sex.
And I would know,
Because she is in here with me.
So, I guess this was therapy.
"Berlin" by Kyle Craft played on my speakers.
I thought about quitting my job tomorrow.
The floating pack touched my elbow,
And I decided I might need some cash.
So, I sank down
And listened to the rest of the song.

Prairies and Prayers

In the west,
He lay wrapped
On the fur of wild game.
Sipping warm liquor
On cold nights
Next to a beautiful woman.
Fighting with words on the page,
No longer needing it to get laid.
It was his whole existence,
The blood and ink consumed his every thought.
She watched intensely,
Wondering if she was his muse.
Like others had,
And others will be.
His mind was too free,
Wild like the setting sun,
And as dangerous
As a loaded gun.

"Got a light?"
She asked.
He reached across the fire lit hardwood floor
Stopping next to the glass bottle
To retrieve the brass lighter

The flame illuminates her perfect features,
And the shadows hide the scars.
They both shared.
They smoke on their backs.
She perks her head to listen
To a tune he hums
From Sturgill Simpson.

Snow is now packed to the window
Freezing them inside.
Harder than new guitar strings
Keeping him another day
Praying this time, he might stay.

Because prairies and prayers are all that we got
When the words fade,
And the music stops.

Pool

Don't save me, I'm drowning
In the pool of broken deeds,
Filled of good intentions,
With a sea of misery.

She stayed gazing,
From a tower built of dreams.
I stayed sinking,
In the waters of destiny.

Destined to sink
Love of concrete
Taking deep breathes
As she crept into depths.

She pulled,
She fought,
Against of what death caught.
I pulled and fought
To hold on to what all I lost.

Don't save me, I'm drowning
In the pool of broken dreams,
Filled of good intentions,
With a sea of sweet misery.

Down,
Down,
Down,
I want to be.

Please, please
Just let me die in peace.
Love can only hold

One healthy soul.
So please, please
Keep yours gold.

Don't save me, I'm drowning
In the pool of broken dreams,
Filled of good intentions,
With a mind of mystery.

Shit, What Time Is It?

Last call was 10:00 PM,
Spent my last euro on gin.
Ushered out into the street.
I listened to words of wisdom,
From an old bar keep.
"Tequila needs no vegetable,"
I threw the lime out and,
"Behold!"
It was there.
Looking through the old bar glass,
She spoke again as time passed.
"Never leave a tab open or love not said."
Knowing at this moment I had to go to bed.
Slammed the shot,
Hugged her once,
Then walked the cold hard streets of youth resistance.
It stuck with me.
When I was home,
I wrote it all down.

Do You Accept the Charges?

I was distant, even when I was close.
Always to the ones who loved me the most.
To the ones I loved,
"You talk too much."
"You're too handsy."
Which always got worse after a couple beers.
They weren't wrong,
Either one,
I'm just imperfect, like most lost sons.
Distance,
It grew between my soul and heart.
Until I only enjoyed the dark.
"It's easier alone."
I would say to the mirror.
Believing things have never been so clearer,
And they were.
It wasn't me,
It wasn't you,
It wasn't our pasts,
Or even the present.
It's the distance between here and there.
Of where we want to be and where we are.
Of where we want to be and who even cares.

A long-distance relation with ourselves
Keeping relations at constant swells.
"I can never settle; I want it all."
A perfect set of
the pride before the fall.

French Jazz

I chained smoked all night. Sipping warm gin out of a tin cup. I broke a promise saying I would stay sober, but I didn't care because a French jazz album I bought for seven bucks played on the turntable over and over again when I threw my empty beer bottle against the wall then another. Anger was a poison I had suppressed for too long. So now it was erupting. The music played on, and I kept hurling empties. Sounded like a country music take on jazz. Honestly wasn't that bad. I liked it.

Dear Future Wife,

I love you. Please, be patient with me. I promise I'm getting better. Just taking the scenic route.

With Love,
Me

Nude Therapy

The after
Of disaster
Is bliss.
It's either one
Or the other.
Touching
Or nothing.
This time, she lied smoking beside me.
She asked me of my life.
Where I grew up,
And my family.
I shared it all with my dignity hanging out,
Something about my mind being numb,
And nudity.
Brought it all out of me.

"Where did you get that hat?"
"A village east of Herat."
"Where?"
"Northern Afghanistan."
"Oh rad. Did you kill the guy?"
"No, not him. The hat was a gift from an Afghan soldier who stole it from a Bazaar. He and his friends looted it."
That sentence stuck and it even made me think. Why had I kept that hat. It was cool, but those guys were kind of criminals hiding behind the might of the American War Machine. But the way that Soldier smiled when he gave it to me. With dirty teeth and kind eyes. It reminded me almost of a child. Like a younger brother bringing you a bully's lunch money. Which maybe it was like that. Yet I didn't share that thought with her.
"You don't talk about it all that much?"
"Don't really need to, it's not who I am. It was just a job."
"What about your family?"

"What about them?"
"Are you close?"
"No, not really, but I call my dad once every couple weeks to chat and check-up. He lives up in the mountains and loves the shit out of me."

I Hate Myself

Locked in the cage
Is no longer hearsay.
It's been months and I still lay.
Waiting for my release
Of these locked thoughts.
My mind tangled in deep knots,
Of rage,
Deep self-loathing rage.
These bars are pressing
Tight against the brain,
Knowing it will leave me lame.
I don't know how much longer I'll last
Running from the Demons of the past.
So, I will complete what I can,
And leave notes for what I won't.

The world is falling down, and I can't save it. All around us there is one sign after another. War, poverty, heartbreak and more and more growth of distance. Distance between each other as we fall back into our shells of complacency and habit. Constructing deep shelters by the second. We don't read, we don't create, we don't listen to music that warms our souls or even take a picture to remember. It's all for people we don't know, that don't care, that will never get us anywhere. All while we ignore the people closest to us, as it grows colder and colder. Until it decays, and we are left alone in our electronic covered box. So I'm paying my tab and heading out. I grow tired of these games. I will find what I need among the people, the real, the true, the artists. To create something new with less of the same. I hope to see you there.

Not Me

I am not your warrior poet,
Nor do I want to be.
I am a writer ,and I want to tell stories.
Not of valor and violence,
But of travel and indulgence.
Too many times has the other been sung.
Too many times my bell almost rung.
Simple man,
Of simple taste,
Do not try and decide my fate.
Listen to me,
I promise it's not worth it.
Chase love,
Chase friendship,
Chase a wild life,
And hone it with all your might.
Because gunfights get old
And most men don't,
I wish I listened when I was told.

Dr. Seuss

The giraffe climbed the tree
To see all that could be
It stared across the sea
And all it saw
Was misery

W Henry Street

It was just before sunrise in Savannah.
I sat on old cobblestone,
Next to colonial homes,
Drinking,
Thinking of how this ended.
She was from New York,
I was from the islands.
She was a doctor.
I was a writer.
We talked of dreams,
Travel,
And some hockey teams.
She asked me,
"Does it get lonely on the road?"
"More than you could ever know."
As the music played on,
We danced to the beat of some reggae song.
After a couple hours the spell wore off,
In a bathroom we decided to head our separate ways.
So, I was walking the streets
Towards home on a broken road.
Now I sit under a surfboard,
At my favorite restaurant
Sipping warm beer.
I hope you'll still think of me, dear.

HWY 96

The stars light my way across the blacktop,
Old country tunes set the mood.
I'm the only car on the road.
This first night of spring.
Cool air kisses my skin,
As it hangs out the window.
Evenings like this remind me of the desert.
In my mind I'm briefly there,
As a take a pull from my flask.
But I'm driving across Georgia
On HWY 96,
Racing from your grip.
I'm afraid to end up like all my friends,
While wishing to hold your hand.
I could drive this road forever
Staring at these stars.

Just Another Politician

Just another promise,
Just another task,
Just another mission,
Just another politician
Saying it's the cost of recession.
I know.
Don't explain me the cost.
I've been here for years.
Fighting behind my tears.
I'm a poor boy,
Led by rich sons,
Telling me how to kill a younger one.
I hate you,
More than I hate him,
Because you care less about our sons.
The adolescent,
Who joined to escape poverty
And oppression.
Just like me.
Red or Blue:
There is no difference
In definition.
To me, you're all,
"Just another Politician."

From The Note

"I need to quit,
But I won't.
Not because I can't,
But because I'd be bored.
I've ruined it all,
Lost my job,
And most things I loved.
All for a couple drugs,
So long."

I chased an orgasm to escape my sadness,
Yet, I was too drunk to do anything about it.
Once again, I choose the wrong coping mechanism.
My friend was dead
From suicide.
Which was something I thought about all the time.
He was young,
Talented,
And had a lot ahead,
But he dove into the drugs instead.
Escaping past traumas like most others.
I should have called,
But I let it go.
Life gets in the way, don't you know.
Humans are selfish,
And I am the same,
Yet, I regret not calling you back that day.

Burnout Underground

Do you hear it?
The tap, tap, tap.
It's the burnouts in the room next door.
Clicking and erasing,
Some might even be painting.
Chain smoking stale butts,
Working all on a project that will surely drive them nuts.
All the way past deadlines,
And not close to being through.
Yet they aren't doing it to please you.
Why would they anyways?
For a couple bucks and a bad review?
So, it can sit on a shelf
And rot with all the others.
While the self-help
And teen fiction
Climb the charts.
No, we are fine.
Enjoy your art of influencers past,
Which was simply just a cash grab.
We will die in the burnout underground,
With unpaid bills
And many cheap thrills.
Because,
Don't you hear it?
The tap, tap, tap.
It's the burnouts in the next room,
Desperately trying to escape this doom.

Fuck you.

Un-published and Unkept

It's well past midnight. I'm watching the rain smash against your window. It was a loud storm, but I enjoyed the sound like a trumpet playing on. I was a young writer who wasn't really writing. Which sucks because I loved the damn thing. I was looking for jobs because I was broke in a dying profession. Thoughts about how empty my bed was rushed to the front while how much I missed her followed close behind. I drove her away because I was mad at the world. I needed to do something. Something cool, edgy, and mine. I didn't want to write for magazines about coffee, I wanted to make art, adventure and love. So, I started writing again.

Here We Are Again

The familiar taste came across his lips.
He had work the next day,
And it was late.
Old memories played in his head,
And her whispers flowed through his ears.
The glass hit the table he built,
For their house,
For their home.
Empty.
His eyes pierced through the old glass
Looking for good fortune,
But found none.
He grabbed a refill,
And came back
To a woman that would never be his last.

It's All Kind of Dumb

Broke the cutting board
Using a knife as a sword.
I bounced around the crowd
With my big black dog
Trying to find the words to this song.
It went on,
And on,
Till we both were screaming out on the lawn.
It's all kind of dumb
This thing called life.
We hurt,
And love,
With structures built on loaded dice.
Which is being tossed by blind mice.
Because at the same time,
No one loves,
They only ever hurt.
We chase artificial highs
To replace sentimental love.
Seeking
Warm embrace with electronic affection
Of virtual drugs.
It's cyclical,
The evidence I share is all admissible.
It's all kind of dumb
Living in this awful slum.

WILDFLOWERS BY THE HIGHWAY

Parked on broken asphalt.
Listening to, "It's my own fault."
I drink beer staring out on the Texas plains.
The wind and the sun sing your name,
And the wild flowers spread
Like wildfires in my heart.
I feel the busted soles in my boots
To match the hitch in my hip.
It's hard to know when you should get off the highway.
Lord knows there is no right way.
If it's not the smokey bars
It will be broken farms,
Or if you're lucky, some old rodeo cart.
Sitting by the wildflowers on the highway
One can almost feel the better days.
Just around the bend,
And a little up the ways,
Hopefully in your arms again.

HWY 20

I love how my mind works when I leave her house.
In that two-hour drive,
I'm everything I want to be.
Passing farm houses
And flowing creeks
Beneath the pines.
Last night,
We stayed up to watch the sunrise.
Just talking.
That's love.
I felt it,
Heard it,
Saw it in her eyes as she said my name.
We walked the dogs when we woke at noon.
I was right where I wanted to be.
I live in that moment
That whole ride home.

Pub on Fire

I saw the end of the world on a bathroom stall.
It smelt like menthol.
It shared no dates,
Or a time,
But I looked at it in a broken mental state.
A Christian man talked to me of Jesus Christ.
I told him I wasn't interested.
It was 1:00 am.
Why did he care?
He then offered me cocaine to consume in a lair.
"Jesus will save your soul," he said,
Wiping the powder from his nose.
Choosing beer instead I listened to him rant.
Men like that draw an audience,
Others came in and he started communion.
I watched the end of the world
In a pub bathroom
From a cocaine preacher
And lost drunk teachers.

Demons in the Taillights

I'm following a line
Of thin red eyes,
On dark corridors
With speckled white lies.
It's quiet.
With background soundtracks
To fill my void,
Of wild thoughts
And condemned promises.
I follow
These thin red eyes.
They pull me in with the siren's song,
Of freedom
And originality.
But,
The demons in the taillights
Rarely tell the truth
Of the lonely road.
And why would they?
Who would follow reality?

Dive

I've smelt it a thousand times,
Heard the roar of conversation more than once.
Music is what separates the greats.
The ones I stay at are filled with
Grunge,
Punk,
And bluegrass.
Cigarette smoke is a reminder of a dying breed.
Reminds me of my grandmother's home.
Where she would sip hot beer,
Garden pineapples,
And smoke Marlboro Reds by the carton.
Dive bars remind me of my family,
Because my family is the company I've kept,
And the blood I've lost in time.
The counter tops stay dirty,
And the drinks stay the same price:
Cheap.

Cobblestone

I've walked every city
From Prague to Baton Rouge,
Honestly like I had nothing to lose.
But wasn't till the second time around
That I was having too much fun.

I hit the ground hard in the ghost coast.
Looking to gamble and maybe to boast.
But that city left me ragged,
And stole all my baggage.
So I left for Texas, with little to no riches.

While I was in the lone star state,
I was constantly planning my escape.
The food wasn't that bad,
But the smell always made me gag.
I'd listen to W.A.S.P on those hot desert nights,
And sing "I'm Blind in Texas," 'til the morning light.

So, I hopped off the train in Northern Virginia
Just trying to find something that glistened and shimmered,
But after a couple drinks I was ready to hit the road.
Figuring this wouldn't be my new abode.

I never learn,
So, I've heard.
Might be my stubborn ways.
Or maybe I'm just still trying to find the right words to say.

SAURE KOMMT HEUTE

My knuckles hurt.
28 was too old for these games,
But pride is always more of the same.
I awoke on a hotel floor,
Wasted in the alps.
A girl I had never seen before was beside me.
A man who was my friend had a busted lip
And laid sprawled out on the couch.
Seemed like a good excuse to grab a drink.
The bar was closed, but I had beer in my bag.
I walked outside,
Unclothed,
In the snow.
Erasing a hangover,
Staring up at the German Alps.
What a life.

A Modern Howl

I watched the declination of my society through poverty.
Not in color or religion
But in bars and casinos.
Fueled by politicians and corporations,
With obesity and depression,
Washed down in alcoholism.
That in a field of virtual interaction.
Nothing concrete,
Just phrases,
And electronic affection.
Slowly,
They declined down,
To the hell of now.
In a place
Molded by divorce
And recession.
Steel walls built up to keep out
What we hated,
Or didn't want to face.
Running never confronting,
Constantly erasing or blocking
Things that cannot be.
I watched my world fade
Into nothing but
Words and screens.

Suicide Note

It's late
And I can't sleep.
I just heard the clock tower chime down the street.
My mind runs through the misty night
Like a kid escaping from petty crime.
The older ones egged me on,
"Hurry, hurry, he's catching up."
It's a boy in his late 20s
With a baseball bat.
My brain tells me I'm out of luck,
You've gone too far for too long.
Heart beat kicks off.
Fighting to survive,
Feeling it's do or die.
An older man grabs my minds collar
Pulling me in tight.
"Do you want to see what will happen when you're alive?"
Nodding back and forth the light flicks on,
Pictures and memories shock my eyes,
Along with all my unfinished work.
Bound in books of thick leather with gold letters.
The old man takes a seat and drinks some water.
My mind then realizes the future is to thrive.
Hands drop the belt of suicide.
Heart beat slows,
Feet step down,
Ears keep ringing but hear sound.
Eyes stare into the broken glass,
It's the mid-20s boy from my past.
"Fuck you, get it together."
"He will."
The voice of the old man chimes in.
Then I drift to sleep again.

Book Talk

"No way it's real.
Not possible to be this way."
I repeat these lines to my reflection at 5:00 AM.
Through little deliberation,
I convinced my myself that I am dead.
Have been for years and
This was just the after effects of my brain shutting down.
My reflection, who is a demon,
Talks the work of books that normal readers,
Ones that are alive in this realm,
Just wouldn't understand.
Like *Green Eggs and Ham* and *The Journal of Albion Moonlight*.
This continued for hours.
The mushrooms wore off,
And the demon faded away.
Sunlight peaked through my blinds,
And the birds picked up their tune.
I called a buddy to ask if I was alive.
He told me to go to bed.

Frostbite

If we survive the winter,
I know we will be better.
At least that's what I tell her.
It's cold
And bitter,
And we have never been quitters.
Frost bites and stains
Things we have laid
At our feet,
Trying to save.
Coyotes howl against the wind.
We promised not to play that song again,
But the amps fired up against the candle lit walls.
Our breath making poison fog
Like cigarettes that we smoked as kids
With wine we stole, with unsealable lids.
If we survive this cold,
Hard,
Winter.
I'm leaving,
Because you looked better freezing.

HONESTLY

I write it all down,
About the repeating sound.
Same old line again,
And again.
Of booze
And should have been.
I hate it.
I hate myself.
I hate these tales I try to tell.
This is the last call on poems,
And honestly maybe myself.
I'm fucking done.

Ceiling Fires

Cold sips of liquor warm my lips
I watch the flame flicker on the walls
Slow acoustic plays in the background
I feel the music in the bottom layers of my heart
It hurts
But it soothes me
Relaxing is the pain
I've never felt more sane
Than under a burning ceiling
I watch the flame flicker on the walls
My rough hands caress your cold heart
You turn away
Awake yet faking sleep
I stare at the ceiling fire
Sipping warm liquor
And embracing the flame

Red Bananas

The light shines
Oddly on the skin
Music fills the cab of the old Ford
I drink warm whiskey
She watches my face
For reaction
Smiles and attraction
It fills me with deep warmth
Like the cold woods by a fire
We talk more
Of life
Music
And desire
I adore this moment
I soak it in
Savoring the smell
Of emotion
And memory
The night drags on,
We touch hands.
The light shines,
Oddly on skin
Of old bananas
And the sound of winter winds

War Bad, Make Me Sad

My body vibrates
To the sound of the music filling my home.
My mind's not in its normal abode.
Candles are lit, and paintings are hung.
I'm dancing around on Persian rugs.
I stare at the book,
The one I read long ago,
High in the mountains,
Snow covered ground
And plywood doors.
Smoking cigarettes on rotted couches
Hearing gunfire in the distance
With rusted tanks
Sitting in the valley.
My body vibrates,
Back to the woman
Asking me about a record playing.
I nod and sip my drink.
Why are my toes cold?

Love and sex are two completely different things and rarely will you find them in the same room.

Afghan Scarf

It's the last of my trinkets
At least the ones of gifts.
A lapis necklace,
A fur hat,
All things I never wanted given back.
They were never bought for a specific girl.
An idea,
That love was waiting back home.
"Once I come back, my life will get better."
Blowing cigarette smoke
Through my wool sweater
To conceal the stench of my hypocrisy.
I carried it around
Town to town,
Camp to camp,
Hoping to make a gift for my wife one day.
"Honey, I got this for you all those years ago,
I waited and waited knowing I'd find you."
It was dumb,
But you need the hope of something
Sometimes.
Especially when luck's not on your side.
It sits in a drawer now,
Years later.
I doubt it will ever come out.

HWY 11

As the plane passes over,
My van maxes out RPMs.
I'm on the run,
Again.
Heartbroken, and mad
At love and a woman.
Two soulmates and not one chance,
It's tragic.
Being alone
And on the go.
I want to share the tale
About the joys of life
And the adventure of time.
It's floating while bleeding.
I'll chase it,
Time and time again,
Because we have to.

The Road House

"There is no god",
My buddy said through a drink.
"Only god ya need is luck."
"That and running shoes."
We clinked glasses to that.
I had drove in that night,
Tired and cynical
From fighting with fate.
This bar didn't care,
My friend didn't either,
He was just happy to see me.
A Jason Isbell song played over the speakers
About how much he loved her.
We all have a "her."
I ordered another beer.

SQUATTERS

He was high,
Sitting in the 4Runner
That wasn't his,
And it was 4 PM.
Heavy metal played through the speakers,
He sipped cold coffee
While snow fell against the glass.
"Where to next?"
He said to no one,
But he had someone
Waiting at home.
Why?
Maybe it's just growing pains.
New town,
New drinks,
New life,
Been here before but this time it was more permanent.
A wild bronc will always crave the plains
Even in Kentucky fields.
Something in the soul.
He flipped the key and turned home.

"The plains are cold
And my bones are slow,
But I flipped the car around,
Passing the pile of black snow
Going toward the unknown and familiar."

Old Town

Homes popping up in places I used to know
The woods fading fast like spring snow
Growth
It's needed, but at what cost?
I believe we are the poison
Stealing the wild dirt
To turn into starter homes
To live next to people
We don't know.
Filling prescriptions
To suppress our demons and steal our ambitions
Going to sleep with lovers
That slowly turn to strangers
Watching entertainment
In cities far away
Dreaming how we will go there someday
While our lives are full of pain
The daily routine just dragging us down
To secure all the things we keep around
In this new old town

Forgotten Cards

I finally unpacked today
From a trip over the holiday.
I'm always late to unpack things
Whether it's my bags
Or my mind
Digging through my clothes
I found two cards
With pictures and messages from our time
Yet it was already goodbye
Because we lived two different lives
Mine, chaotic and strange.
Yours, normal and sane.
My mind processing nothing but pain
From a life I made
I regret nothing though
Reading the message, I knew
I was better off to lose.

Fuck, Your Eyes are Beautiful

Blue,
Deep crystal fucking blue.
I stare at you like a painting,
Something constructed for the world
To appreciate and understand beauty.
How did you find me?
I ask that on days when I'm clacking away.
Trying to figure out what this characters supposed to say.
I stop from time to time,
To look at the pictures on the fridge.
You,
With those fucking beautiful eyes,
I want to see my reflection in those one last time.

There It Was

She was simple.
All she did was care for me
And enjoy my hobbies.
We were honest
And open.
It was love.

It was fun while it lasted.

Seven Years

I want you to know I got better
Through the hard times and liquor.
Along the road of broken past,
I found something to make me last;
Love.
With the places I escaped to,
And in the words I scribbled about you.
With the voices of the lost
Nipping at my spine,
I found it hard to write.
In shadows it's hard to see
Something worthy of memory,
Something to make me happy.
I would have never made you happy
Not enough to stay
I know that now.
Yet I never understood,
Til' I battled with my own demons.
Attempting to fill busted walls
With broken glass
Discovering it was all just full of rats.
I set a fire to my tragic past,
Standing in the flames to burn it all away.
I want you to know
I got better
Through love.

Dream Journal #531

My dog was following me through the woods. It reminded me of Oregon, with the tall trees and the wet grounds. I watched his black tail bounce in between the ferns as he stopped occasionally to look back at me. I carried the old repeater rifle, hunting for a better path out but knowing it was dangerous to leave salvation.

Then I saw the white tail of the wolf bounce and leap. I swung the stock of the rifle and connected with its shoulders. The wild beast knocked me to the ground biting ferociously at my barrel. When I looked in its eyes, I saw nothing but white-hot rage and my reflection. My dog was nowhere to be found, so I fought alone. I pushed the rifle into the wolf's mouth like a stick, driving forward instead of back. Falling onto my knees I made one final push while simultaneously swinging the rifle around. A single shot rang out and ripped through his back leg. He stared at me, doing nothing, having no reaction. He turned and limped back into the growths of the forest as silently as he came. Then my dog bounced back to my side. I woke up

HYDE

The voice in my head won't let me sleep.
He keeps going on about jazz,
Talking to girls at the bar,
Reaching over to grab drinks.
Scat, scat, scat.
His voice rattles off faster than I can keep up.
I can't get a word out but I keep thinking of lines,
I'm scribbling shit down.
Yet he is getting louder and louder.
"Why won't you let me sleep?"
Is it to keep up with some consistent beat?
I don't know,
Yet I can hear the crowd against the glass.
The faces make shadows against the white powder,
Reaching out as the band plays on.
I shout "no, no, don't come in!"
Yet the door flies open,
And the bartender ushers them to their seats.
Lights go out,
Music stops.
I hear claws across the bartop,
It pulls me out of my terror with screams.
Who was that voice that wouldn't let me sleep?

Chefs, Writers & Painters

All creatures of the same sickness
Wandering artists
Creating masterpieces
From nothing.
Whether it be,
Paper,
Pen,
Or knife.
Working for nothing,
Living off scraps,
Just for a chance
At everlasting life.
Not for themselves
Vanity has no place in art.
To live,
Dream,
And die.
All just to help others cry.

Worn Out Blues

I was too broke to travel
But just lonely enough to dream
Living on meals solely based on agony.
Working just as much as I would barely like
Then cursing at the boss man for my lousy life

God Damn
These worn out blues

Silence filled the hallways
Like the drink down in my glass.
And I'm too stuck in my ways to let go what's past
It's probably not helping staying on the bar stool
But I figured, what else I got to lose?

These headaches come and go just like leaves do in the fall
With the ringing in my ears sounding like a coyote call
Sitting on the porch I swear the wind would scream my pain
Or maybe it's that long black train

God Damn
These worn out blues

I always wanted more
Even when it was outside my means
Then that same old thing would sadly become my dream
Slowly I'd watch it slip away
Like trout do in the stream.
Not from lousy luck but just me being too fucked up

God Damn
These worn out blues

You came and went
Like whispers in the rain
And I can't help but cry about the things that I can't change
Sometimes at night I scream out at the stars
But my voice never reaches all that far
Probably cause you've been gone too long
So, I'll sit down and just write another song

God Damn
These worn out blues

Van Life

January 30, 2020, Boone NC

It snowed last night so I know it's going to be a great day. Surprisingly enough I stayed pretty warm in the van overnight — think it got down to 19 degrees. I spent the night in a Lowe's parking lot believe it or not. The national park was closed due to "extreme ice." Yet it was still pretty beautiful. Something about the dark parking lot surrounded by the mountains underneath a clear starry night made it seem like the best spot I could find. Surprisingly enough that little candle I have heats this place up pretty well when you need it. I do feel like I need one more big blanket though. I wasn't cold at all but one more would make it just right. Might put the big fur one in here for trips. I'm glad I came on this trip, it reminded me how much I love doing this. Getting out on the open road just listening to music, ascending up in the mountains with the snow sprinkled tops. Recharges your batteries in a way not much else can. I'm going to make breakfast, have a cup of coffee, then drink a nice cold beer right before I hit the slopes. Because it snowed last night and that's how I know it's going to be a great day.

Runs through the river
Straight through the trees
Strives to be wild
Just like me
Black as the nights
But he cause no fright
Just like those damn demons in the lights

Dream Journal #27

Thorns protruded from the ground grabbing at all passing life. Almost as if to reach out denying passing to these fields of death. You felt the weight in the air of the devil's den.

Seeing lands of infinite death makes you focus on your own mortality. Thoughts drift to what were or could have been for the warrior spirit, making you want to hold your loved one close and never see battle again. It's sobering like black coffee with a cold winter gust, chasing your lips and rusting your bones. Dread and respect are the only emotions that fill your heart. Then you leave.

Border Towns

"I will never be nostalgic of this place,"
I thought to myself on the way out of town.
Desert heat ripping through the ceiling
Of my rusted white van.
Yet I am.

It reminds me
Of when we started.
Palm trees hiding the moonlight
Keeping us company at night.
Sand trails
With mesquite trees
Remind me
Of us.
Competing
Running faster
And further.
Always seeing who was better.
Looking forward to us
Being together.
I miss the heat
Licking my skin.

Always Another Round

It was dark on a Sunday night.
My friends were in the back seat
Screaming a Beastie Boys song we had been singing
For two days.
We were fucked up and out of control,
But on the edge of 30 that's the way it goes.
As the lights passed through the windshield,
The music blared.
I felt the true fear of mortality.
It seemed like this would be the last great time.
I gave up hope in the passenger seat
And grabbed a beer from the back seat.

End of an Era

Things I never really share
Linger in my brain.
Usually pushed back,
But tonight, they are on the attack.
Recently, it's been a full invasion.
Why,
Why now?
Changing times,
Changing tides,
Maybe a couple lies.
Like,
I don't care.
So, I share little from that time,
Because it's mine,
And those who were there.
It's only ours to share.
The children of the gods,
Strolling with six little monsters.
Maybe ten years from now,
I'll tell those tales,
But
Probably not.

A Cold Day in Hell

I'm stuck between love
And hell.
My dog can surely tell.
He watches me cook all night sometimes,
While I pause to write.
Something I'm working on,
Legal pad
After legal pad.
Papers all over my desk,
Words become
Kind of a mess.
I want to quit,
"It's ruining my life,"
I scream in the freezer.
My dog just rolls over,
"You can't stop now"
He says through a grin.
"You're too damn close to the bloody end."
He was right.
So I tossed him a bone.
One poem about the past,
One about the present.
It will be a cold day in hell
Before I learn my lesson.

Why Can't We?

Why can't we?
Why can't we lie on the floor?
Play that song,
Dance in the kitchen,
Hold each other till the next sunrise.
That would be too formal,
I guess.
Or,
We could give in.
Make grilled cheese
At 2 am.
Sing old ballads to each other in the tub.
Sip on cheap wine
And laugh about good times.
Why can't we just do this every night?
Why can't we stay in this moment?
Why can't we make it work?
Why do you have to leave?
And why am I talking to myself?

Short Dreams

I fell asleep to the sounds of gunfire
That some kid was watching on his phone
Of a fight far away.
The bursts of machine guns
And small pops sounded close.
I sank into an old couch
Deeper and deeper.

Waking with my face covered in thick mud,
My heavy pack pinning me to the ground.
I couldn't get up.
I fought harder and harder but it pinned me down.
I stared at a danger marking, of an IED.
Orange lights forming a circle around.
The sound of mud sucking boots to the ground,
Trudged by,
Towards the unknown.
Grabbing my own machine gun,
I made a life depending push.
I was free.
I got in file.
The mud sucking to my boots.
I trudged by,
Following them towards the darkness
To what I have known.

A tug on my shoulder pulled me out.
I felt the cold on my shoulders and pain in my legs,
Staring at the discolored carpet,
My mind was a whirlpool
The edges of my vision blurred.
"Are you okay?"
....
"Yeah, kid, I'm good."

The sound still emitting from his phone,
He was maybe 12.
As he walked away, I whipped my eyes.
Why do my fingers smell like mud?

12 Grams

I ran through the woods last night,
Naked,
With the foxes.
Rain soaked my skin.
I came across a house,
All the lights on,
Boxes half packed,
Food molded on the table,
Pictures blurred.
Rain picked up and I stood under the overhang.
The house was halfway
Between the living
And the dead.
Weird,
Soon the foxes called me back.
So, I chased them back through the woods.
Guess seeing all I needed to see.
The street lights came back on,
And I was home,
Cold,
Wet,
And wondering.
Why were there no doorknobs on that house?

Boring is the death of love
That's why we keep hooking up

Okay, But Why?

Why not?
I'm horny and in love
With things I can't be with.
I'd rather have it this way.
My heart belonging to one,
My body to others.
Keeps me in the specific mediums.

No Need to Rush

As we fell apart
The back dropped out of our life.
I saw explosions of dying passions
Like a nebula.
Pulled by the saving of lives
Against the grips of legions.

Everything is lonely.
Everything is bullshit.
Everything will die.
All these will be crushed by the weight of time.

While we hide
In self-made tombs, that were our homes,
Filling it with trinkets and friends
Yet to just be stuck alone again.
Self-doubt is a drug best never kept
Or washed down with a bottle of regret.

No need to rush towards the end.
Half of us aren't ready to face our sin.
And why should we?
We spent a lifetime ignoring it.

Beat Up Toney Lamas

Busted boots and blown out tires
Seems to have a common outlier.
Running towards or away,
Chasing white lines
Washed down with petty crimes,
It all blurs together after a while.
Bought these boots in a small border town
For 600 bucks, no money down.
Treated them in cheap beer
And whiskey tears.

These beat up Toney Lamas
Sure could tell a tale
Especially that time we spent the night in jail.
It's heartbreaks and who you know,
Out here living on the road.
So, keep your tires right and boots on tight
Or you won't see another night.

From honky-tonks to cobblestone
We roamed this land
Shortly after I bought the van
From a police auction in Laredo.
Locked away for dealing Amphetamines
1200 dollars then she was free
I loved the way those tires sound on the road.
The three of us make a great pair
Cruising up and down I-10, with no luck to win.
Chasing half pint dreams
On half broken wings.

These beat up Toney Lamas
Sure could tell a tale
Especially that time we spent the night in jail.

Its heartbreaks and who you know
Out here living on the road.
So, keep your tires right and boots on tight
Or you won't see another night.

Don't know if I will make it.
To the shows in Las Vegas,
But the lights keep me driving through the night.
If I crash and burn, I won't be hurt
Lying bleeding in the poor man's dirt.
Because at least I had the guts to live.
How many people can say that?

STEW

Stew is such an easy thing.
Meat,
Potatoes,
Carrots, butter and broth,
But you can use water instead.
I made it once,
For some poor boys in the woods.
Rain was slapping against an old tin roof
Soaked from sleeping in an old storm drain.
I was 16.
One of them pulled me out,
We made a fire in a state park bathroom.
The six of us sat wet, just trying to get warm.
All hungry, we collected the bits of food we had.
I offered to make stew,
Because I knew how.
We ate in the silent light of an old bulb.

I hope those guys are doing well.

Horror

Fungi
And some pizza pies.
Not your normal combo.
Watching old horror films
To relive
My Blockbuster youth.
Slasher films
And old wine
Reminds me of 99.
When I meet my mother
For the first time.
Cinema was just a generational excuse,
The eternal Friday night
Filling it with PG-13 fright.
Babysitters hunted,
While we were unattended.
Us watching screens,
Screens watching us.
Television supervision
Is a generational excuse
And continues to the next.
It's our safety blankie
Like the comfort of streaming your new murder mystery.
Binging,
Binge drinking
While swiping
Until you have nothing.
Ain't that scary?

Reset

I woke up naturally.
My dog looked up from the foot of the bed.
He usually never lets me sleep this late.
Today I made my own coffee,
Then I did the dishes,
My apartment looked unkept
Like a modern art display.
She left a polaroid on the fridge
"Call me again for more of the same xoxo"
Good sex will reset the brain.

Soundtrack to that Night

Crackling of a fall fire
Crickets of the night
Would be the opening song
Laughter and sing alongs
Would follow
On the soundtrack of that night
Bottles clinking
While we should be sleeping
I guess we were already dreaming
Abandon the tent
We are paying the stars rent
As our bodies made a melody
Intwined for a short time
I lost my mind in the song
Before I could say "so long"
Behind the wheel I smile
Packing my old sack for a little while more
Your song played in my head
Again and again
Then the soundtrack began

Back on the Grind

I attempted suicide
Twice in one week
From sadness.
Eluded by my creations,
They seemed all the same,
And I was completely drained.
I wrote in the dark,
Like how I got my start.
Locked away with the weak
Creating a prison
Of music and books
Sorting things out for a third look.
Then,
I found a rhyme
And I was back on the grind.
Saving myself a little at a time.

Going Through the Life Cycles of Self-Care and Self-Destruction

Crushing pills
Then pouring it in my drink
All to try and finally sleep.
Fuck me,
Why did I become this leech?
All I wanted was the white picket fence,
But I craved the chaos,
And you can't have both.
Canceling flights,
Dodging life,
Just to document my demise.
What a shit experiment.
50's rock plays
While I try and pull it together.
It breaks me open like an earthquake,
But I just drink again.
I hate me
And love, "love."
Which is as real as hell itself.

Another Round

Blank pages
Stare at me
With empty beer cans keeping them company.
Just another rough night
Trying to be the best I am.
Something I didn't think I'd survive
Unsure why these are my best moments.
Not for sanity
But for words
And art.
Just trying to escape
Myself,
Love,
Pain,
Just everything.
Another round
In my hand.
Another round
In the chamber.
Another round
I don't want to remember.

Standing looking at wine bottles
Listening to Damien Jurado.
Odd for a grocery store to play this.
Sometimes when I'm feeling lonely,
I go here
Just to walk among the people.
I write the date on a bottle
Then store them in the cellar
For the next time
I feel like this

Went West

She talked to me of her boyfriend
As I drove down the city roads.
Taking swigs of the bottle,
She grabbed my thigh,
I kept my eyes on the road.
I didn't care for her
Just an escape.
We made love that night.
She traced my scars with her finger tips.
The music from the bar below
Shook the floor.
I listened
While she talked.
He came from a broken life
Trailers and addicts
Life with bad habits.
Just like me,
Just like her.
Endless cycle, I guess.
She spoke more on abuse,
From fathers
And cousins.
My heart hurt for her,
I held her tight
As tears soaked my shoulder.
"I wish I could make it all fade away"
Whispering through whisky breath
And I meant it.
Truly, I did.
All hurt souls want to heal the other,
Because we know why we wander through life.
Even if I didn't know her last name.
I drove her home in the morning
Sharing cigarettes and bad coffee.

Having every intention of seeing her again,
Don't know why but I just had too.
Yet when I returned next Tuesday,
She was gone.
"Went west"
The note began
And I never saw her again.

Foreign Porch

Looking up from my lakeside porch
I noticed the stars looked different.
"Ahh different hemisphere, different formations"
I mumbled to myself
As music played on.
I was alone
Drinking shit beer
And smoking expensive cigars.
Nothing out of the ordinary,
But I was abroad
On a porch that wasn't mine,
And I felt like I was the only man in the world.
A geo citizen
Who else would notice
Different star formations?

Groceries

This is an odd process for me.
I'm not completely used to refrigerated food storage. Walking through the aisles, I pick up the meat, cheeses and vegetables I enjoy to cook with. I watch my peers of similar age pack baby formula and Mac & Cheese. It reminds me of how unready I am for the next step of life that is reproduction. More than likely, I will have to throw out some food because being on the road so much it goes bad in my not so visited fridge. Checking out I chat with the woman behind the register. Small talk. She comments on my bottle of wine, I ask if she wants to come share it with me. She laughs and continues to ring up my items.

Danced to Death

She clocked in through the back door
Never completely sure
When it was Thursday to Monday.
Peak times.
Changing in the back room,
She looked into the mirror
Wondering if this was ever ending doom.
Yet, she liked it
In its own way.
The rush,
The life,
The drugs,
The temporary love.
Passed down from man to man
Dollar for dollar.
She slides down the steel bar
Rotating for paper value
And new opportunity.
No different than we all do.
She danced to death
Every night she could
Trying to reach the other side of the bridge.
The source of happiness and love.
But,
She died in her car
With a needle in her arm.
Completing,
The dance of death.

Low-Lit Street Lights

My tank is almost empty,
Phones almost dead,
Slow country song playing through the speakers,
And I'm almost out of beer.
Tires repeat that steady rumble
I'm singing that song at the top of my lungs.
I love the road.
Low-lit street lights guide my path,
From place to place,
Bed to bed,
To smiles and memories.
Fuck, I hate leaving my friends
And their warm homes behind,
But they know I will come back.
I always do.
I'll fill up in the next town over
Crack one last beer along the way.
The low-lit street lights are calling me home
And this song just keeps playing along.

Ashtray

Sitting in my rusty box
My mind goes back to words we talked.
Soft hands on hard skin,
Hoping to feel again.
She held
Onto my soul,
Refusing to let go.
I begged for her to stay
Knowing it was my only saving grace.
Yet,
She left
For salty seas
And new memories.
A place I once held dear
Now I remember with warm beer.
I miss her
Auburn hair
And revolutionary smile.
It shows me
I won't see it for a while.

Heartache Road

I've drove this highway twice,
Once in the summer
Another in the winter.
Thought it would end in a different place.
Still hit the same bumps
Ran out of gas in the same spot
Even stopped at the old rope swing.
It's heartache road,
Where I go to run from the blues.
The beginning and the end
Are always the same
And I never know why it always rains.
123,
11,
63,
I remember all the streets.
Curves of the mountains
Give me the highest highs
And lowest of lows.
I bet even you know,
Heartache road.

Short Stories

Dying on the floor
He sipped.

Phone tone stopped
Also, his heart.

Film reel flipped
Burning the screen.

Souls connected
Still, it was destined.

Heartbroken,
The bathroom smelled of sulfur.

Did I do something wrong?
No.

He promised to change,
She left.

She held hands,
That weren't his.

Beach Release

Explosions
Fade from illusions
Built from psilocybin.
Erased my mind
On sandy dunes.
I doubt it's an awakening
Just more shaping
Or releasing.
Some form of
Outer body.
Tall as hell and deathly skinny,
He picks me up internally.
"Are you ok?"
He says with a sonic boom voice.
"I don't know yet but now I see the choice."
"Good, little man."
He then throws me back into the buried sand.
I'm up to my neck and my friends stand with shovels
"I guess I caused a little trouble?"
"Yeah, asshole, you wouldn't stop running in the ocean
And trying to read to turtles."
Fair.

Lies

I like the sense of entitlement veterans have,
How they remember it was all about service.
I like how social our society has become,
All these social media companies really did the trick.
I like how my neighbor's dog
Wakes me up every morning by barking at strangers.
Just like I'm sure he likes
How I keep him up late with my guitar.
I like how easy it is to get mind altering medications,
And I really like how expensive it is to go on vacation.
I love the music I hear on the radio.
I love the books that are popular now.
I love the media that keeps us afraid.
And I love politicians telling me what to say.
I like how single moms have to work two jobs
And deliver take out to keep a roof over her head.
Probably because it reminds me of my childhood
And keeps me warm.
Did I mention I like veterans?

Close Out

I watched the spiral blue light wrap around my beer. It was a Friday night so normal for the connection. Marcus was loud, and I sat sipping gin. I thou

Depressed and Undressed

I thought about suicide tonight
To the point I'd thought I'd die.
It hurt
Watching the faces of loved ones
Cry over caskets.
Yet that was a memory.
From a time with me
Alive and believing.
From a moment I can't stop living,
Then it all sunk in.
I didn't need the has beens,
I needed hope.
With a sprinkle of compassion
The ever-mortal sin
Breaking open the mold
Words cracked my mind
I told you the toll
It was your soul.

From a trash cup wine
I heard Goralski,
Odd sounds from a plastic cup.
Locals surrounded me with foreign tongue,
It bothered me none.

What is 'It'?

What causes these deep thoughts?
For weeks it's all tasks and completion
But,
Late one night after a couple glasses of pinto
You contemplate
Everything.
You desire legacy,
Children,
Homes,
Love,
Comfort.
You pace back and forth,
Thinking, "have I made the right calls?"
Yet you're not even 30.
What do you know of right calls?
But you know everything,
Because you are young
And saw the world once over.
Loved hard
And lost twice.
Fired shots in anger,
And others in stillness.
Walked hard roads,
And climbed tall mountains.
Yet,
You know nothing at all.
What causes these deep thoughts?
In my opinion it's simple,
Fear,
Doubt,
Pain.
You will never rid yourself of these things.
They are just life.
Being self-aware is a pain in the ass,

And you know that.
The only cure of it all
Is to live your life without risk.
Even at the top you have doubt,
Or you wouldn't be here.
Tell that girl you love her,
Move across the country,
Quit your job,
And live life fully.
Make you happy!

That Makes It All Worth Living?

Have you ever made love
To a stripper
In a graveyard?
I have,
She has two kids now.
But that night,
We talked
Music,
Life,
Love,
Books,
And art.
She enjoyed her work,
And I did too.
I held her hand
Walking among the graves.
I loved her
For a fleeting moment.
She left me.
Sad,
With nothing,
But sweet memories
And grass-stained jeans.

10 PM on a Tuesday

My dog is telling me to go to bed,
But he has the same voice of my dead fiancé.
It scares me,
I hear the echoes down the hall
And stumble to the kitchen.
Refusing to look into the bedroom again,
I see bright pink blood spill to the floor.
My back against the wall,
I slide down,
Grasping at the now.
Clawing out of the pit of the past,
Hearing the cries of my former self drives me to the corner.
Pain,
Like a wounded animal
Or a dying child.
I look down on him from the catwalk,
He looks too young,
Face too smooth.
"Why damnit?"
I scream into my memories,
Slamming the ice-cold gin.
I stand up,
Shaking the memories like a cold storm on the Atlantic.
Finding my dog on my bed I pet his sweet head
Smiling as if I had come back from the dead.
Ice clinks in my full drink
I pour it out.
What dreams may come tonight?

Driving Lightning

Spent off wine
I rolled down the highway
Through the storm
Trying to see it my way.
Irish folk music was on the radio,
The lightning in the sky caused its own show.
Consuming a psychedelic at a gas station,
My brain hit its perfect serotonin
With the peak of the storm.
Watching the electricity fill the sky
I believed I would never die,
And I won't.

I noticed most of my friends falling off the dirtbag lifestyle at this point in my life. Either going to get higher education or settling down. Taking real careers to take up root. I was even guilty of it at times, living in an apartment filling it with things and living in the tangible realm. My soul screamed at every moment I spent working and in the real world, begging to break free, begging to be back among the trees with the stream. So, work for me at that age was just a way to save money so I could leave again. I would have to find new friends to accompany me on these wild adventures which was the worst part because I really liked my old ones.

Black Cadillac

Throw me in the back
Of an all-black Cadillac
So I can listen to the blues
One last time.
Me and the driver will swap songs,
Turning it into a real sing along.
Halfway there,
He will turn that thing around
Knowing I'm not ready for the cold hard ground.
We would hit the road, him and I,
Touring the country from side to side.
The driver and the corpse are up to no good,
Just trying to sling some wood,
Or bone, if you would.
So, when I pass on to the great beyond,
Throw me in the back
Of an all-black Cadillac,
And God damn,
Don't let them play
Fleetwood Mac.

Rock Bottom Again

I promised to quit drinking
But I took a sip
Writing this
Just slowly
Losing it again

I should buy a home at rock bottom
Because the weather isn't bad
And the people are the right type of sad
I could be the mayor
Walking around doing favors
Breaking fences
Tearing down stop signs
All to make it better
They would all know my name,
Saying "damn what a shitty guy"
I'd smile and wave
Just enjoying my day

Guess I'll stick around for a little longer
Because some promises
You have to keep.
So, I'll look at bus routes out of rock bottom

Not So Inclined

Started a band
But only one can play.
The others are just taking up space,
All just trying to make a dollar
Or get laid.
I'm just trying to bend these strings
To heartfelt melodies.
Maybe write a song
About love
And drugs.
Or the love of drugs.
Something I can hide the meaning,
So people will listen.
Because people don't read,
Nobody cares,
They all just want to focus on the me.
Narcissistic,
Idealistic,
No artistic reach.
But who gives a shit?

I was writing down poems behind a desk at a Super 8 motel. Dingy, broken, and dusted, coming down after a concert. I felt extremely rusted. The booze and the mushrooms were wearing off, but I felt the emotion in my heart as fresh as it had come. Fuck, I love this terrible life.

Late Fucking Nights

I stared on God's face last night
He looked like Kris Kristofferson and Buddy Holly.
Music playing in the background
Confirmed my fears of reality.
It didn't exist,
Nothing was real,
But the conversation I had was true.
When death brings its final rhyme,
I'll remember these times.
I've seen all I need to see.

Scotch

Back again
Spinning back around
Was up but now
I'm just back down.
Guess you can say
I didn't learn a thing
But how to embrace old pain.
I'll cut myself off this time,
Not going to fall into
My same old trap.
Not growth,
Just limits.
But I'll probably light another smoke.

Superstitions

Cut my foot on a broken nail,
Right before I was thrown into jail.
Should have saw the writing on the wall,
Should have ran to make one last call.
Trusting my gut rarely steered me wrong.

Earlier that evening we were pressed against the wall,
I felt the creation of God in your touch.
Like your sweat was ecstasy,
And mine was LSD.
Stars exploding as our bodies collided,
Bending sparks across the room.
You brought me to my knees to pray to you.

Superstitious of commitment
I left her house as the sun set.
Love punch drunk
With nowhere to go.
Leaving early, surely cursed me.
Shortly after I lost my wallet,
Then found myself in a bar room brawl.
Boss called to tell me I was canned,
And the cops were looking for me and my friends.
They caught up to us a quarter to two,
And I was thinking I'd call her up.
She was probably asleep
And not thinking of me.

Running from the law of societal acceptance. Parking in a different place every morning on the island. I hope they never catch me.

ABSTRACT

The love of passing rain
Wet,
Dry,
It's all the same.
Comes and goes
As quick as it flows
Down the pipe
To who even knows.

Just like summer flings
With wedding rings.

Every troubled artist is trying to make something truly great before they leave this earth. The trouble is keeping themselves alive along the way.

Tattoos

Someone asked me
"What's the ink mean?"
I told them
"It's all distant memories
From a time
Or a place
Or a lover
I can't replace,
So
I take a piece
With me to keep"
To remind me of
The good
The should
And
The, "would I do it again?"
They keep me here.
And the
Burn of the needle on my skin
Keeps me grounded
To the when

Payphone

"I don't know where
I got to go
To get a fucking break."
I stayed on the phone
Begging for home.

Cash in the Good Book

Foot bouncing in a church pew,
Thinking about what all I'd rather do.
Preacher man talks about salvation,
I'm wondering why God needs my donation.
Big guy upstairs can create the sky,
Why does he need my two last dimes?

Church ain't nothing but crooks and thieves,
Reminding us how we are the worst of the seven seas.
You can set my church on fire,
Build me a place full of earthly desire.

Roll out the carpet and fire up the band,
I'll start touring across the land.
Bringing music and wine,
Spreading the gospel of a damn good time.

The crowds would grow as the tent was erect
Knowing their place in eternity was surely set.
Bring me your hot, open, and willing
We don't care if you have no shillings.

Because at the Church of Love
We all get down.
You can ask anyone around,
We stay up late, and sleep through the day,
And will never bother you on an early Sunday.
So come one, come all, I'll show you around.
We owe allegiance to no crown,
No gods, no kings.
Not even a cross.
But I'll be sure to save you a spot.

Good Times

Shaking my head
Like an 8 ball for different answers,
The river's babble fills my ears.
Tossing old pictures in the fire,
I keep a couple
Just to keep my edge up,
Especially when writing stops.
I'm going to find my way out
With the road under my feet
And the music in my heart.

Thump thump
Thump thump

My home is everywhere I feel new things.
The past never gave me any comfort,
It whipped me raw
Leaving scars and making me skittish.
Like a wounded dog on the farm.

Good times to me.
Used to be women and booze,
Shit, sometimes it still is.
Now it's tires and gas,
Woods and laughs,
Rock and chalk.
Maybe that's moving on,
But I'll keep this picture to remember it all.

WORDS

Philosophers and scholars
Made words easy to rhyme
Like "moonlight"
And "bright"
They sure are kind
To lost souls like me
Finding rest stops
In words
And stories
Helping me along
Life's long journey.

Philosophers and scholars
Knew what words were meant to be
Like "you"
And "me"
With misery.

Nobody is bigger than death. You would be ignorant to believe any one life is worth less than your own. The youth are the only value. After that we are all just burdens of society unless proven otherwise by unique contribution.

Cocaine and Tears

How many beers
Do you measure in tears?
I'll add a gram,
Some powder
To slam my mind
With hot emotion.
To make it all louder,
Accelerating my mind
To reprising important times.
I honestly don't see this as a crime,
Just therapy,
Not as bad as ketamine.

Paris

I wish I was the one
To take you to Paris,
But it was him
And now I hate it.
I've chased the city
And the spectacles,
But your memory has ruined it.
I see a wine shop
And I think of that red we shared.
Pass Jim Morrison's grave
And that record we listened to plays in my head.
Us sprawled on the floor,
Reciting lines and sharing theories.
Back then I was too poor,
I still am, honestly.
"Living by the art" will do that to anyone.
Still,
I knew we would have fun
In the city of lights.
It should have been me,
Instead of that boring man.
I was just too busy playing music in the van.

Oklahoma Just Outside that Casino

The whining hum
Of a fluorescent light
Rings on the patio of a dive bar.
I smoke stale cigarettes
And sip water beer
Listening to locals
Bitch about the times.
How it's all going up
Drug prices,
And property taxes.
Odd,
All I was asking about was my bar tab.
The whining hum
Of fluorescent lights
Matched with the strums
Of an old guitar.
In a fire station,
That sold beer
And created good lines.

Camden

I was walking the streets with a Canadian man.
I can't remember but I think his name was Stan.
We went from bar to bar,
Doing bits on "The Canadian and the American".
Stereotypes from both or countries,
I'm fat.
He's polite.
My country likes war
And his hates bud light.

A British girl cut in,
Telling me my president sucks.
"Lady, I don't even vote"
"Well, it's all your fault you stupid bloke"
"Next time I'll vote for you"
"Well, aren't you just bloody rude"
I didn't understand.

The next day I played guitar for a punk band.
I looked in the crowd and saw my British friend.
"This next song called, Voting in Bed"
She threw a full beer at my head.
After the show she was waiting out back,
We went home and had a full-frontal attack.

As I smoked a cigarette out the window
That morning I thought,
"Where the fuck is Stan"?
I never saw him again.

Lazy J.

We shared passion filled nights
In the back of my old van.
Listening to songs about turtles
And watching the lights change.
We consumed psilocybin,
Listening to the river whistle through the rocks.
You bent down to grab my…
But,
A scuba diver walked by.
He gave me the peace sign.
I looked to see if he dropped his fins,
But all I could see was three yellow hens.
"Oh yeah we are on the farm"
I whispered while you held my arm.

The One I Didn't Plan

A sexless and emotionless relationship
Will drive a man to sobriety.
At least it did
For me
Most nights.
Stress and shame caused from nothing,
But my heart.
Guess it's payback from the past.
At the peak of my existence,
Things were slowly falling apart.
So,
I played.
Ringing of the strings,
While singing offkey,
Soothed my mind of raging storms.

"For it was the one I didn't plan,
That drove me mad.
To make something I didn't think I had"

Shit,
That's not bad.

Fireflies

Can't remember the last time
Maybe since my childhood
I watched them dance in the grass.
Hot summer nights
To make time pass.
That was when my family was whole,
But that broke long ago.
Yet,
With the return of the firefly
So is my life.
A woman who loves me,
Some simple poetry,
And makeshift family.
A star shoots across the sky
As the crickets
Make sounds in the night.
I need no wish,
Because I'm here.

Gin and Eggs

Gin and eggs leave a strange taste in your mouth
Like rubbery orange juice.
The bus takes off,
My eyes roll around in the cerebral liquid.
Sunlight reflecting off the windshield
Drowns out my vision.
The music in my ears drowns out my thoughts
I miss my home,
Yet enjoy the rolling stone.
It's a double edge,
Finding my own form of comfort
In each hand.
Just like gin and eggs.

Office

My favorite place is a bath
With an ice-cold glass.
Sidney Bechet playing through the home,
Staring at a painting of a turtle doing blow.
I sip, rocking to a tune,
Patiently waiting for you.
I scribble on my papers.
The smoke from my cigar fills the room,
It tastes like Havana,
Where I picked it up not so long ago.
I hear your wet steps through the hall,
Ice crashing against the fresh glass in your hand.
I love spring,
But this ain't my home
And that ain't my wife.
It's sadly just my life.

She flipped the pages, peering into his mind. "Wow," she whispered. He worried it would push her away. His deepest fear was loss. He knew this after all these years. A fear imbedded him since his youth, that was driven in over and over again by a hard nomadic life. Yet for once he didn't want to push away and run. He wanted to stay and face this new life. See his mind had worked in so many places, so many roles and times that he grew accustomed to turning things off. Flipping switches in his mind that channeled it elsewhere. Not anymore though not this time.

It was his only exposure to compassion.

Calling the Kettle Black

No relationship is typical.
Anyone who says otherwise is a fool.
They are simple in a sense,
Just few listen.

Be happy
With who you want
How you want,
However you can.
That's it.

C.C. Me In That

When people die
They are always great.
Did no wrong
Lived a great life
Was such a beautiful soul.
Yet what happens
When a great man dies?
It leaves a black hole
In many lives.
You will sit in your car
Watching raindrops slide on glass
Thinking of times you shared drink
Think of times you should have called.
Yet,
That doesn't matter,
Not anymore.
Because a great man died,
I hope his memory stays the same.

Cold Nuggets

Day old beer
Just like before.
Don my robe,
Light a smoke,
Every day is more of the same.
I eat cold nuggets
Hoping to numb the pain.
Unsure of why,
To be honest it's kind of all the time.
I just hate,
Me.

That crippling loneliness, the type that leaves you in bed for days. Trying to dream your way into a different existence. That feeling of nothingness, it's a hard drug on the mind that has no stimulation. It will cause creation if you can survive though. Yet sometimes I'm tired of surviving it, I'm just cursed.

Red Well

Jazz
And pizza.
Danced on the tile,
Quoting lines to classic tunes.
I poured a glass
For you.
Spilt.

Mood Right?

I met a girl
Who worked at a western bar.
She was a poet,
Who lived in LA,
Through her words she had a lot to say.
I wondered what brought her here,
As we shared a beer.
Then a shot
Or two
Til' we decided how we lived.
Two bumps
Of cocaine
Made our night.
As we kissed beneath
A fading street light.
Guess we all
Share those lonely nights.
Fuck, I hope she is doing alright.

Fires

Cigars and wine
Fill with passion
And engulf the mind
Shared between two,
But not to begin
More of
A tradition.
A dance
Of silent, unspoken romance.
No touch is needed,
No wine lips shared.
Just company,
And illicit affairs.

Lucy

I realized normality
In the eyes of a dog of everlasting memory.
I watch punk rock bands
Scream against the sands
Of lyrics most don't understand.
Sipping wine,
Oppressing time
With an old German Shepard.
I can learn a lesson.
Things are not as lost,
It's all about the next fetch.
Toss the ball
And bring it back.
Lucy like a diamond,
In a sky or some shit like that.
But I'll still remember a dog
With more love in it
Than a girl from Georgia.

Rupi Kaur and Other Micro-poets

We sealed a pact.
Not to time
Or fate,
But to our souls.

"New place
I'm probably not safe.
Lonely night,
Might go look for midnight delight.
Lovable
Jessica, kept me alive.
Beer for bed,
Nothing left to be said."

Expansion

I spent the night listening to music and drinking. I wrote a couple jumbled words along the way. I hope you enjoy them. Maybe I wrote these same words before. But I probably forgot how it went and I'm saying them once again. Shouldn't that make it more important. More severe. Like you had to listen. You had to understand. Because if I had to say it twice it had to mean something. I think I'm stoned.

Talks with Patty

Bearded man
Telling me tales of how times had been.
He spoke the wisdom
And bought the drinks.
He said,
"Write
For your heart
And what you have lived
Because people know the difference."
I never saw him again.
Well,
Until the next time.

Too Damn Young

The open road always felt like home to me.
Maybe because as an adult running that was how I solved issues. Not really solving anything, just delaying or never facing. So, like that the road became a limbo. A place between destinations where your mind can wander. Music will fill your ears and you will think about your best and worst days. A farewell, a kiss, a lover turning away from you in their sleep for the last time. The road has no answers, but it is comforting. Put-put-put the sound of the tires as you drift, bring you out of deep thought. Crack a cold beer from the six pack you bought two states back.

As the liquor processes in my liver. Thoughts process as well. Memories become cold flashes of entities. Like rain on a hot Sunday. I can't explain how, or why. But the taste of it all seems so familiar. Yet maybe that's just the gin. She lays next to me as the moon reflects off her back. I think I'm going to leave in the next five minutes. She could rock me off course. No doubt in my mind.

The Weight of Love

We are inevitable
Like particles from meteorites
Pulling each other in
To predetermined ports.
Just destine souls
On the journey of life.
How lucky we are to share it together.

The weight of love is like gravity,
It's heavy and light.
At the same time,
Love is a black hole
Pulling everything
With destructive force
Giving you the chance to float.

I'd do it all again,
To have my bones crushed by love.
Ripping away the very fabric of time,
Leaving me in the dark unknowns of space.
Because in that vacuum,
A star dwells in the far corners of the universe.
I can feel its heat,
Pulling me in.
Wanting to start again.

The weight of love is the cosmos,
Exploding into a billion directions.
Bringing life to millions of planets.
Circling around their own orbits,
In their own galaxies.
No two stories are the same.
Love, bringing air to these homes,
Helping things grow.

Flourishing,
Colliding,
Surviving.

All from the weight of love.

Packed Cars

I really think there is something to say about someone driving down the highway with their car fully packed. A far away place and miles on the road. Are they chasing a dream or running from somewhere?

Women are the sole reason men wish to survive on earth. They make life better and we are grateful for them. Holding the hand of a truly great woman will make a man's week. To kiss that same woman, a month. To be loved by a woman that fills your heart and makes you not just want, but helps you become the best possible version of yourself. Well, that will make a man's life.

I Thought It Was Clever

I have been death.
I have been creation.
A nightmare
And a king.
Lived in villages with not a soul in sight,
Also, in cities with big bright lights.
Drinker,
Gambler,
Traveler,
And even a lover.
But most people call me
Music.

With Time

What can you do with time?
You could take a walk,
Maybe even twice around the block.
With time,
One could share a gentle touch
Or lose a lover to perpetual lust.
But with more time,
You could change it all.
See with time,
Nothing is certain.
Except that we have a lot of it
And that it goes way too quick.
So,
Read,
Travel,
Drink,
And love.
Do everything you must
To use all your luck.
Because like time,
You can never get it back.
So, enjoy the life you have.

Reds

Hot summer nights and cigarettes,
That's what sex smells like.
Memories,
Sprinkled with self-hate.
Night sounds,
Providing background music
To your inner thoughts.
It's damn terrifying.

The Law of Conservation for Passion

Some loves aren't meant to last forever,
And that's ok.
Passion is like matter.
It cannot be created
Nor destroyed.
It exists forever
And always.

When it fades
It does not cease to exist.
It just hides,
Flickering,
Waiting.
Til' that one song ignites a spark,
And you remember nights lost in time.

Passion is forever.
You remember it from its smell,
And the taste is like sweet red wine.
Savoring the flavor,
Clutching,
Holding,
Saving.

Saving for those lonely nights.
The cold black,
Starless ones.
It will keep you warm
With hope.

I'll cork it,
Shelve the bottle.
Keep it for a rainy day.
Because I love like matter,
And it will never fade away.

Silence the World

My neighbor shot the birds
As they sang out to the world.
The sky was black and red,
And then they were all dead.
God damn.
How come?
Why did you hate that song?
God damn.
My son,
Why did you fire that gun?

Must have been angry at something else.
Because I heard you scream at yourself.
Saying,
God damn.
How come?
Why did you take so long?
God damn.
My love,
I knew you liked that dove.

The porch grew quiet after that,
And the door slammed against his back.
Soon after I heard a shot,
And multiple shuffling cops.
Saying,
God damn.
A crime,
This old man lost his mind.
God damn,
How come?
He chose to silence his world.

4/5

This day usually sucks
Lingering like winter ducks.
Like those ducks,
I'm usually alone.
Locked away in my cabin.
Scribbling away on old linen,
Listening to musicians almost forgotten,
That share this day.
It's our day.
One of beginnings
And endings.
Together we march through the halls
Boasting on our great calls.
"We did this."
"You should try that."
I just nod my head and laugh.
"I think I'll take this one fellas",
Then I'd strum on my guitar.
"How about y'all just head to the bar"?
Then they would scurry out
Going on a spirit walk about.
And I'd be alone again,
But the music played on.
And I played on.

Lame

Fuck who you want
Fuck them that see
Fuck everyone that told you what to be

The man comes down to make you see
Their corrupted philosophy
Technology teaching the kids
Of the new improved way to live
While the parents gulp pills
So impressionative

Fuck who you want
Fuck them that see
Fuck everyone that told you what to be

Medication now rules the nation
Go find a new mental health representation
Out in the streets
Down in your homes
Could even be someone you love

Fuck who you want
Fuck them that see
Fuck everyone that told you what to be

How did this become my reality?
Sure, couldn't have been violent TV
That was last millennium's bid
Maybe it was social distraction
Built while we were looking for action
Then we had zero reaction
When your screen built a democracy
Saying

Fuck what you think
Fuck who you are
Fuck, you better tear each other apart

Oil Slick

Far across the trees
A hole keeps getting deep
And the blood I've tried to stop
Has only gotten brighter

And the moss screams to me,
"You won't have long to see"
Yet I can't even run
Because these men carry the guns

Dead man's eyes stare black
Like that old black cat
Who already ate his lunch
And I think I have a hunch
What will feed the bat

The hole is way too deep
And the blood is at my neck
The men have tried their best
To take me out in peace

And the cat I tried to feed
Has gone to drink his mead
So, the bat will stay and watch
As the dead gain a notch

THURSDAY 9:45

Whitemarsh Island

I'm running late for a party so I'll make this short. Nothing is more powerful than music. Some say smell is the most powerful memory stimulant. Yet I don't believe that's true, at least not for me.

"Pain", by War on Drugs, plays through my speakers on a late-night drive. I flick my cigarette out the window after one last day. It brings me back to road trips. Winding down mountain roads while you tell me, "Shut the fuck up and listen." I hear it now, now that song is haunted. Like many songs. The album "Southeastern" by Jason Isbell sits on a dusty shelf. Its grooves filled with ghouls; its sounds filled with the pain of the boy I used to be. It's the sound of me learning to play guitar and fighting to survive my mind. A new chapter began for me after that, and it's still being written. Just like these damn songs. In the basement of my soul colors roar to the sound of music. It leaves a strange road map on the floor guiding my life. It adds emphasis to all our lives, creating background noise to the scenes of memories. Even if it was never there. Preserving them in time like old whisky in an oak barrel. It's beautiful watching it play in our minds, saving it for the next time.

Golden Tubs

Stay still as I wash the black bear cub.
He is wild and not thrilled.
Still, I keep him.
Because who else will?

He only drinks wine
And never wants to be dined.
Unless it's raw meat,
Which makes sense why that's all he eats.
Efforts of domestication, I suppose.

Still, I try.
Even after he got outside
And ate at that poor boy.
I suppose he thought he was a toy.
Which is easy to mistake with Nephelium.

So here I stay,
Trying to teach this bear cub
The right things to say.
In the Golden tub
With lots of love.

Infant of Prague

Something definitely doesn't belong
When you see an infant walking the streets of Prague.
It's what I thought about in a show in North Carolina.
I read it on a sign from a worn-out church
Wearing my cleanest dirty shirt.
A parking lot turned to sound
Behind a van and a greyhound.
Singing rhymes
About burnout times
And sipping warm beer
Out of grimy coffee cups.
We definitely didn't belong
Just like an infant in Prague.
But that's kind of the point.

Land Before He Sea

A man with no home
He's tired and alone.
Trying to play
All he can say.
Before he breaks lease
In the land before he seas.

So close to done
What has he begun?
Destined to lose,
Yet that might be the booze.
Spinning misery,
With land before he seas

Parked on this land
Of forgotten sand,
Yet it's not all that bad.
I sure hope you're glad,
He found madness
Beneath land before he seas.

Waves form the rocks,
Yet he ain't on top
With what it creates.
Even though he moves
Like a fucking earthquake.
Just mating like bees
With the land before he seas.

Painted like a clown
Especially with the crowd.
Still, he wears no smile,
Because he knows it's vial,
And it will make him feel worse.
A final decree
In the land before he seas.

GOD'S A CUNT

Why else would make this rotten bunch,
Yet maybe we deserve it.
Worshiping new false idols by the minute,
Made of flesh, not gold.
Who live high on some Hollywood hill
Being famous for just being famous.
While journalists pander for the government,
Making constant news, that is just constant noise.
The old man in the clouds would be proud,
Of how easy we will condemn the poor,
Sick,
And broken.
Locking them in corporate penitentiaries,
So, your 401k will have a 2% gain.
In God we trust,
Ain't that a bust.
Yet we are living in God's country.
The new religion of politicians.

Orange Piano

Passed by on my way to buy a used guitar,
Mid-day drinking was a great start.
Saw it on a quick glimpse
In the window of a big white mansion.
Unplayed,
Unkept,
What a shame.
Orange pianos
Need to be played
Like old records
And spring ball games.
I imagined hosting parties in there.
Fancy food,
Expensive drinks,
Surrounded by people I didn't like
Just trying to make my place among these socialites.
"We are so excited for your next book!"
"You really should come out to our house next weekend."
"It's almost yacht season."
I would smile and laugh,
Faking my way through my own home,
Wishing I was drinking beer alone.
The orange piano would play on and on,
While I would drink another one.
All the hits would be played
"Bad, Bad Leroy Brown"
"Crocodile Rock"
Maybe even sneak in the "Sultans of Swing."
Nobody would know the tunes, and I would be miserable.
That's what the high class gets you,
But we all want the orange piano in some way,
Even if it will ruin yesterday.

But what do I know?
I'm just on my way to buy a used guitar.

Roadside Rope Swing

Stopped for a break
On the Blue Ridge Parkway.
No other travelers,
Just I.
Came across an old rope swing
Above the mountain stream.
How long it had been there?
I did not know.
It reminded me of my youth,
On other forgotten creek beds,
Where we too would swing into depths.
I missed those days.
Should I go for a swing?
For old time's sake?
No,
Better to not partake.
So, I hit the road.

That One Night You Still Think Of

She was the opening line to an all-night bender.
I made love to her by the side of a river.
Her blonde hair gripped tight in my hand.
I knew we would never see each other again.
"You have no soul,"
She whispered laying on my chest.
I didn't understand, nor contest.
"Not in a bad way though," she continued.
"Just trying to read you is like staring at a blank menu."
"I get that all the time,"
I replied sipping gin.
But I didn't.
We made love again shortly after.

There are two truly beautiful drives in America. Blue Ridge Parkway through North Carolina, and the desolate desert road of Route 66 from the Grand Canyon to Mexican Hat, Utah. Both must be done at day break when nature is more alive than man. Don't be too shy to stop and have a cup of coffee at a stunning view. You won't regret it.

Feelings

I stayed up 'til sunrise.
Drinking
And playing
Sad sounds.
It's my favorite feeling.
If you add a little drugs
It's better than making love.
Funny thing is,
I can't recall,
What I started writing this song about.

Napkin

Old bar tops
Tell stories
But few listen
They see the scuffs
And the stains
But not the pain
Not the end of the road
Down on the luck
Drink till my last buck
They only see
What they wish to see
Or what they want to be
Listen closely
You can hear the future
It says
You will get better

Sobriety

I slept in a cold metal box
Packed in like wet wool socks.
No drink for me,
I needed to see.
I've learned over time
That's when things go wrong,
It's best to have a clear mind.
So, I don't drink when I'm upset.
Makes no sense to ruin a good buzz.
Why waste the booze on sadness?
Drink to make good times better,
Not to sit with sad letters.

Talking to my Demons

Pour a shot,
Talking to the mirror.
"You really shouldn't play that song again,"
My reflection says, smoking from a cigarette pipe.
"Well, what the fuck do you know?"
I reply, playing my guitar from the floor.
"More than you do sadly."
"Well riddle me this, all-powerful entity."
I strum along from the bathroom floor,
"Will I finish my album?"
"Only if you don't kill yourself first."
He might be on to something.

Prompt Too

This is a wonderful life.
I'm alive,
I'm home,
And I'm well.
Surrounded by friends and family.
I find myself happy,
Guess it wasn't so bad after all.

I didn't drink
I didn't write
I just sat around in silence
In the prison that was my mind

Evelyn

"I have always admired painters,"
I said sitting on a stool nude.
"I bet you have, I've always liked musicians,"
She said from behind the canvas.
"Maybe I'll write a poem about this."
"I thought you wrote songs?"
"Songs are just poems with repetitive verses and music,"
Then I took a sip,
"At least to me they are."
She stood behind the canvas thinking on the subject.
Her blonde hair tangled in a mess
And sticking out from the sides.
"I like that, now stay still."
I listened.

The Last Heartbreak

"Luck is relative
And luck is 90 percent of it all."
I was warned,
Yet I never listen.
One,
Two,
Three,
And at last, it wasn't me.
I hate caring.
I'd walk away but,
I await to find the words to say.
That is the definition of insanity
And this is my last heartbreak.

Drinking with Ghosts

I spent the night at a roadside bar,
Trying to figure out if I went too far.
Wasn't the plan,
But here I am,
Just another casualty of man.
The ghosts in the graveyard kept me company,
Swapping tales of misery.
They told me to let go of hate
And embrace fate,
Love ain't a game for saints.
Ghosts are funny like that.
Speaking in riddles and never truth.
Telling you that there is no absolute.
Hurt,
Not mad,
Just sad.

Drunk & Happy

Solid title
With truth.
A brand-new gospel
Got me feeling like a tent revival.
A combo I thought wouldn't match my youth.
Young but old,
Or so I'm told.
But we are youthful,
Drunk on emotion,
Happy on chance,
Let's take this dance.

January 15th

A bridge on the outskirts of Brownsville, Texas.

I threw my gun into the river trying to ensure a less painful demise. Slamming the bottle back till it was empty gave me a little relief. Hoping I would just pass out or die. Calling out has been done before so I won't be a burden this time. Pushing people away has become a second language to me. I'm tired of being tough and alone. It's exhausting. I'm tired of bringing new people into my life because I don't know if I have the strength to carry on. I'm worried I'm going to let them down; I'm worried I'm going to fail them like she failed me. I don't want to be around anyone, I just want to continue to exist alone.

Honestly, I deserve it.

Stetson Surfer

I knew this man in south Texas. He was a rancher born and raised. Yet he loved the sea. Every morning he would tend to the cattle and drive over an hour to paddle out. Religiously almost. Like a Sunday sermon but more serious. I first noticed him by his hat. A big black ten-gallon walking through the sand and an equally big board under his arm. He would place the hat wrapped in a towel on the sand and hit the waves. He would place a beer can in the Stetson to weigh it down. The Stetson surfer was a phenomenal rider. I watched him for a good hour just enjoying the art. I stopped him on the way out and got his story. We drank semi cold beer on the tailgate of his diesel. He came from a long line of Stetson surfers. His grandfather had taught him to surf as soon as he could swim. Teaching him the beauty and respect of the ocean. While also teaching him to rope and ride on the ranch. His great grandfather learned to surf in Hawaii during the war and just brought it back with him. Passing it down through the generations. He told me, "There is no more peaceful of a living, riding the ranch and riding waves. You are surrounded by nature and at mercy to its will. You will never control it, just enjoy it for what it brings each day." That stuck with me and I don't think I will shake that. He changed out of his board shorts and into his Wranglers, packed a can of chewing tobacco, and took his beer to go. I would see him a handful of times after that, always having a post session beer but eventually my ramblings got the best of me and I found my next town. I've never met another surfer like him, and I hope it stays like that. Compared to him, you are all kooks. Long live the Stetson surfers!

Bad Habits

I have a carton
I bought in Mazar-i-Sharif
For 10 bucks and a beer.
I've saved it for about a year.

I have a bottle
I bought today
For 7 bucks I made off a fight.
I've finished most of it tonight.

I have a song
I play over and over
For no reason other than to feel.
I've done this for 6 years at my heels.

I have a heart
I listen to way too much
For the lie that it's the best thing to do.
I've learned more than once it's not.

I have a pen
I keep for company with my sin
For it's the only way I know to heal.
I've been doing this for 16 years.

I have bad habits,
I keep them close,
For I know that they keep me well.
I've been this way for far too long.
And I plan to keep going strong.

Sitting here
Drinking in my van
Writing stories
About times
I should have been
I thought I was at my destination
But then I lost it.
Somewhere between mile marker 25
& 29
Yeah, that seems about right
I'd turn around
But I'm quite tired of looking at the ground
Wondering why it's not looking up
I'm sure I'll find it at the next stop

Gutters

This world is a rotten place.
That gives no shelter to the maimed.
Born broken and you will be tossed aside,
To sulk in the darkness of your mind.
No matter how shattered,
The human soul stays the same.
It craves a gentle hand,
Soft words,
And adventure to stay sane.
I've seen the lost and broken,
In every corner of this world.
Hands reached out, yet not for more.
Just an escape of where they are.
I do what I can,
Yet carry them all in my heart.
Because I too was broken,
Wide open and left apart.
I wished for kindness
At the depths of my heart.

HOTEL BACKYARD

I used to stroll this abandoned lot.
Smoking cigars,
Drinking cheap wine,
Sometimes play a game of baseball.
Lived in a makeshift jail cell,
A cheap hotel.
Isolation due to government rules.
I went mad in there some nights,
Trying to find the will to write.
Until sunrise I'd fight the good fight.
When the moon was high,
I'd go to the backyard,
Just to sulk and think of better days.
I did 11 months in the Holiday inn,
Then I was back in the salt air.
Back at my bar stool,
With my surf guru.

Marshians

On the islands,
There is a tale.
That predates the men that walk its sand.
Spirits in the marsh,
Calling,
Like sirens in the night.
Beckoning,
To the lost,
And damned.
I hear them through the marsh,
Welcoming me
To join them.
I bring a glass
To appease their thirst.
But,
Seems like it's just for me.
We all sit by the fire
On these haunted nights.
Trying to resolve
Old fights
With demons,
And ghosts,
In these damn forgotten coasts.
On cold autumn nights,
We touch the void
Between the worlds.
It's good to see you, old friend,
Hopefully it won't happen again.

On the Counter Again

She dropped down to reach a bottle,
He sat behind an old barstool throttle.
She saw his face and lit up,
"I was wondering how long it'd be till you showed up,"
He smiled,
"I've been too far gone, wandering around from here
And beyond."
"Sounds like you need a drink."
"How did you know that was the link?"
They stared at each other,
Not speaking but remembering.
Emotions lasting not that simply.
So they drank,
And they laughed,
Enjoying a memory
From so far past.

This Time

If it doesn't work out this time
I'm passing off to island life.
Because there is a genie in a bottle,
That I just have to swallow.
Instead of wishes, she's erasing minds.
Though I'm filled with ambition,
I know it's empty living.
My heart can only take it so many times.
Old flames are an existent fire,
That not even salt air can retire.
Go for broke,
Till there is no hope.
Love with courage,
Because what's the alternative?

Grape

The most dangerous weapon is that cigars make wine taste like grape juice. Wine with no flavor, causes no pause. No pause when drinking causes good times. Good times... well they can be dangerous.

Poetry Contest: Subject, Milkshakes

I wish I could make you quake.
I stand there on the cobblestone,
In a certain, *end of state*.
I love you,
But how can I break my thoughts?
I know my time is drawing near,
I am aware we are almost out of beer.
I can and will find you again.
I want to elope with you on desert sand,
But roads are broken and filled with holes.
I know it's hard to journey through the snow.
I will freeze my heart,
I will wait,
Until we can meet for milkshakes.

RGV

Been alone with nothing but thought and music.
Only companion I had was melodies and tunes,
And the beats treated me well.
Keeping the silence at bay,
I probably didn't have much to say anyways.
Luckily, I had some paper to record most of it.
Ink and alcohol share the same viscosity.
Lucky for people like me.

Future

I don't know if I'm running away or still discovering myself. I'm 26 and 38 at the same time. Born to run, but still stuck in the middle with you. Oldest young man. I should probably keep a better journal or just keep writing. Maybe I'll be a teacher when I retire.

Border Madness

I can't take the heat no more,
Coyotes always right outside my door.
I believe this place is driving me insane,
But I might have myself to blame.
I stay up all night,
Staring out into the desert's bite.
The cacti are his teeth,
Sharp and pointy with scraps of rotten meat.
Cheap tequila surely doesn't help,
I've personally heard it make mutes yelp.
It's rotting my brain,
But most definitely erases pain.
I'm losing track of days in this border madness,
Might be the sunshine,
Might be the sadness,
All I know is I might need a Baptist.
I've been gone too damn long.
But honestly, that might be the perfect song.

Ronnie Dunn once said, "I'm lost and found
In a border town."
Now I understand.

Woodland

When I was young, I played soldier.
Dressing in old fatigues
From a surplus store.
I would dive into the trees
Head first.
Sticks for guns,
Playing "Fortunate Son."
The pines and vines
Wrapped around my mind,
Teaching me their language
In the wood lands.

Hunting came later,
Looking for deer in late September,
I learned the value of life.
As I grew,
So did the trees.
Somehow, I knew
They would stay with me
In the wood lands.

I would trade hunting for hiking.
Enjoying the nature,
More than the rifle.
I sought adventure still.
Not wanting to trifle with books and pens,
Off I went to join a few good men.
Thinking I would become a man
In my woodlands.

I never wanted to write,
I just felt like I needed to save myself.

TRAZODONE

Dark showers.
Black rain
Simulated, to initiate thought
Or reset pain
Hot
Unknown
Feel the wet stone
Audible ring
Lingering in the steam
Silence
Smells come after that
You smell cookies
Even though you know it's not real
Eyes tighten to eliminate any light
You can smell apricot lotion
Getting closer
Audible ring turns to muffled voices
You shuffle though the ghosts
Heartbeat races
So close
Water turns hotter
Then you lose it
Slipping away with the water down the drain
Slap the water off, feel for the towel
You have forgotten her voice
And it's all you chase

Nocturnal creature on the Mississippi bayou
Come on baby if you want to

That sounds like shit

Fake Tropics

Why do California palm trees look so fake?
Skinny, thin, flexing in a gentle breeze.
They appear to me the thought of a paradise,
More than the truth of it.
Helping people believe this is where they all belong.
"California Dreaming," is more than a song,
It's a cult anthem to sway the masses.
Once was the day where it all was true,
But now that is as far away as the moon.
The dream has busted larger than the Hoover Dam,
Leaving depression and poverty to flood through the streets.
Your beauty is still there my dear.
I see it in the eyes of every screenwriter.
Will the fake tropics fade away?
Revive the glory days?
I do not know,
It might come after Santa Monica's next snow.

741

As above, so below,
So the story goes
Lore and myths
Wrapped behind a religious kiss
Crowley spoke of these things
In his manor
Built by Archibald Fraser
Sober for 6
Will summon the 12
Even the very dukes of hell
Free to roam upon the land
To lend rock and roll a hand
Hosting the Sabbath
And turning the page
With the words that we all say
Sing
741
Against the eclipsing sun

Red Fire

"Let's drink and sleep all day."
Words whispered around mid-day.
Red hair and skin poking through sheets.
How the hell did we even meet?
You roll over and smile,
Ask if it's been a while.
It has.
Longer than most,
I'd rather spend my time alone,
But I'm sure you must have known.
Sometimes I need saving from my own.
One night can bring you life,
And light a fire deep inside.

APRICOT
THE SMELL BRINGS IT BACK

Aging

I looked at pictures of people I went to high school with. They were having kids getting married, working in offices, and having dinner parties. I was loading gear, planning gigs, writing rhymes, and checking on other men if they were prepped for the day. This is all I had known my whole adult life, other than my time in the Army. Which was more of the same. Just trading guitars and pens for rifles and ammunition. I didn't complain, this is just how I choose to live. But I still wonder what it would be like on the other side. Maybe I would live in the Suburbs, drive a sedan, and have office friends I meet for poker every Thursday night. Carry a briefcase instead of a guitar. Have a wife and kids instead of a van and drinking habits. But then I would always wonder what was on the other side.

Tuesday, 12 PM

Savannah, GA

"I didn't know you came here too?" I looked up from my drink and there she was. We had history, but it had been awhile. A year or two maybe, I wasn't sure. She pulled up a seat and ordered a drink. No one was there at this time of day. Noon was only a time for the real drinkers with a problem to marinate in thought or hangovers. What she said next was something I anticipated. "You never called. I didn't think you would, but I had hope somewhere in the back of my mind." With work how it was, that was normal. Yet she was truly beautiful, the special kind that makes you stay past last call and dwell on the whole next day. I was still there from the night before, still thinking and dwelling. I paid my tab and left without a word. It was too early to deal with reality. Some things are better left unsaid and she was better without the words.

Dreams

I had a dream I had a son
He was 6 and I never knew him
I felt the fear of losing him
Wanting so bad to just be a part of his life
I awoke and that fear lingered
I decided I did not want children

Payphone Blues

A matchbook
And a quarter;
Isn't that a classical scene
From our childhood
Memories?
Slam it down,
Draw a smoke,
Having a conversation with some old bloke.
About coffee,
Or wine,
Or some women who lost his time.
Yet he feels for her
When the rain comes down underneath his shirt.
He looks up and stares at
Black,
Cold,
Rain,
And it makes him feel sane.
So, he takes his matchbook
And a quarter
To bother another old soldier.

LE CAFE

A woman told me today,
"I will always love you, but I gave up on you long ago. I know I can never get you to stay in one place. It's not who you are." At first, I disagreed but then I knew she was right. Every attempt I've made ended the same.

I get restless.
I move on.
Like some old song
Chasing some adventure
Or something wrong,
Some place where no one knew my name,
Yet ending all the same.
I guess it was at that breakfast,
At some cafe,
That I realized
I was lying to myself.
I was the problem in my loneliness.
It was me.
Like a mustang in a corral, it wasn't meant to be.
And that's ok.

My best thoughts are always when I'm hungover. I want to quit drinking so much but it's when I get my best work done. Who would give that type of creative spark? Addicts have said this, I know I'm not far from it.

I'm dancing with the devil.
Trying to find words,
that will last forever.

Molecule of Madness

I held the molecule of madness in my hand,
Riding at night against those cold desert sands.
It kept me warm,
And fought against the storm,
Even if it kept me hidden from our lord.

Before I knew it, I was just south of Spain
Fighting with the man that was trying to cause me pain.
He stood six feet tall and held a pipe of lead,
His eyes pierced black and soon I'd be dead.
Come to find out,
He was living in my head.

Oh lord,
Oh why,
Can I never die?
This molecule of madness is rotting me inside.
This song,
These blues,
Keep me running across the land
Looking for a reason to keep up with the band.

What drives a man mad?
What makes a man sane?
I will tell you, it's just more of the same.
Drink doesn't help,
But its's rarely the source of pain,
And love can wash it all away
Like a hot summer rain.

Yet the cause
Of the molecule of madness
Is simple, my friend.
It's just desperation

Mixed with sweet depression.
So go try your luck
Against the man in your brain,
Because the poison is brewing,
And you keep on losing.

Oh lord,
Oh why,
Can I never die?
This molecule of madness is rotting me inside.
This song,
These blues,
Keep me running across the land
Looking for a reason to keep up with the band.

Boarding Call

I like a short-haired blonde with a barrel racer draw
And I loved a red-haired girl with tattoos on her scars.
I once felt fear and lust,
Sitting passenger to a woman with a vintage muscle car.
I guess you can say,
I love a dangerous gal.

SOBER

A month without
Binge drinking, strange.
Used to think
The booze
Made me crazy.
I realize
That is not true.
That's just how I aged.

Travel

I've spent my life in search of the perfect bar. Many times I thought I found it, and then another would change my mind. I used to think it was the food, because we all get hungry. Then I thought it was the company, because after all we all get lonely. Then I found that sometimes I just wanted to be alone. Drinks are all the same, prices are the only thing that changes. So what makes the best bar? Location and time. How it makes you feel at that place and time. That's how you know. If it quenches your thirst for what you need and fills you up, then it's the best. Luckily it will always change. So you will never be too far away.

Are you a poet or an imposter?
Well, I'll tell you I'm not a lobster
But if I was, I'd be a blue one
Rare and unique
But I'll admit
That's a little bleak

House

The pitch peaked
At the moment our eyes locked
We twirled on carpet burned toes
UV lights radiated the walls
The flames rose up our legs
Singed our hands
Scarred our skin
Grips tightened on our bodies
And lifetimes passed between us
We erupted at the second chorus
Super nova
Leaving no energy for an encore
Resting our bodies on shipwrecked shores
While some song repeated by *The Doors*
As my vision faded to black
I felt your hand
Grasp mine
Coming free from your blouse
I knew
That we were just playing house
On borrowed dimes
And broken times

I Hope You Hate It

We chase artificial highs
To replace sentimental love.
Warm embrace is words on a screen
Of virtual drugs.
No real connection.
All byproducts of our adolescence.
Top five changed by the day,
Of friends that changed on the words we said.
So we keep up the tradition
With followers and subscriptions.
Only now we ignore the words from families,
Replaced with the affection of strangers.
Who would complain?
Who would cry?
"Not I,"
Said the lonely man.
"Not me,"
Said the empty misery.
We dive deeper,
Seeking a meager cause.
All because we have already lost.

The Road

People are afraid to leave the comfort zone,
But me, I welcome the unknown.
The could be,
The mystery,
"The will this destroy me?"
Adventure beacons to all of us.
Late at night, while we lay restless in our beds.
The open road reminds us we will soon be dead.
We roll out with the morning light,
Planning routes that will make it all alright.
From one highway to the next we will roam,
Chasing someplace that will feel like home.
But we have already found it,
This place we call the road.

Animals in the Clouds

Look at the clouds, I'm seeing animals.
An elephant eating a flamingo,
Can't remember the last time I saw that.
Like a child on the grass,
I sat and laughed.
Enjoying the pleasures of imagination.
Where did it go all these years?
Was it washed away in liquor tears?
Or maybe it was just my subconscious fear.
I miss the springtime sunflowers.
My grandmother growing them in clay pots.
I'd lay in the grass and watch her tend the crop.
"You can't plant sunshine in shit."
I always loved that bit.
I grew older,
And she did not.
But I still think about that old flowerpot.
One spring evening I heard her say,
"Watch the clouds they will tell you your day."
"If it's an animal it means good fortune,
Oh, look I see an elephant."

Simple Was Death

Simple ruined us.
It made us look for excuses.
I'm too tired.
I'm too fat.
I'm too special to deal with all that.
Yet we type on our phones how upset we are.
Dealing with emotional scars.
It became too easy to see the better.
It became too easy to feel inferior.
It became normality to live in poverty.
So we hustle with the bustle,
Hoping to escape the luster.
Not of fame or fortune,
But of deaths and misfortune.

90's Country Song

I needed love
Like a 90's country song.
Something about the lonely barstool
With the mysterious woman made sense.
A convertible Cadillac,
Cutting through the Appalachians.
My broken heart and their soft skin,
Made me want to be a better man again.
We would run from the law,
With stolen cash in her bra,
All while I sang songs from a broken jaw.
That album would play straight through,
While we made love under a neon moon.
Just making promises we knew too good to be true.
The chorus would hit,
And we would be beside a lake.
Cold mountain water wanting to decide our fate.
I want to love like that country song,
Make me feel like I belong.
Just hope the journey won't take too long.

A City I Shouldn't Love

They said it's full of crime.
For me I'd probably never find a better place to die.
Surrounded by the art, the hungry and the believing.
All hoping that this is the end of the yellow brick road.
In the city that never forgets to raise your rent.
That' where I like to stay spent.
The conversations are better,
Even if it is just about someone's editor.
Here we all secretly believe it will get better,
Knowing we will have to leave next year.
But at least we have good food.

Guess I'll Write

It feels later than it should.
I'm stuck beneath the West Virginia woods.
I like it here,
Even more than lukewarm beer.
You know,
The type that sits on the wooden table
As you sit with an unmoving pencil.
The fire cracks and yawns,
While you go search for another one.
That other thing being a replacement
For a decadent arrangement.
You hid it deep in your heart,
Saving it for that special spark.
It may never come,
It may never last,
But you sit there trying to bring back the past.

My Small Desert Friend

Does the scorpion always walk like that?
At the ready,
With the tail curled back.
Or does he let his hair down at times?
Crawling around the dirt next to those lost dimes.
Finding solace in the aging metal,
Enjoying the light that the sun must give him.
That burning reflection,
With those cold dead eyes.
Or do you think he just wants to fight?
Maybe the scorpion
Is the last cowboy.
Destined to roam the earth with no real joy.
Just stings and pinches,
As he scurries life through the ditches.
The desert heat,
Radiating anger through his feet.
I may never know,
Just like when I try to understand the western snow.
But next time I see my small desert friend,
I'll hope to see him again.

Best thing of 30 is you got 40 years to 70.

WILMINGTON

I sit beside a dark pond,
My drink is essentially gone.
Beneath the Spanish moss,
I recollect things lost.
The night owl sings,
As moon is shining,
And the fish leaped at something I cannot see.
But I sit beside this dark pond
Beneath an old tree.
Writing words, I'm sure no one will read.
Then,
A star shoots across the sky,
And a splash is heard in that very sign.
So I know,
You were here with me.
I down my drink that is now completely gone,
And head back home,
To ponder the beyond.

Last Page

Once the sun comes up,
I stop to care.
You leave without word,
I shower with my favorite album.

At night I'm begging you to stay,
Calling and asking you to come over,
Believing in love,
And praying you do too.
But in the morning,
My work is the only thing that matters.

These damn words
Are my life.
I want to create more so I run away
From everything that could ever change
The way I feel about my work.
I did once,
Some could argue twice.

I'll never do that again.

To the Academy,

First of all I'd like to thank my editor Keith. The fact that you are even holding this book in your hands is a direct success of him talking me out of getting rid of it a dozen times. Without him and Tyler this book would have never been finished and for that reason they will always be my friends. Also I'd like to thank you, the reader. Without you the written word would cease to exist and be replaced with a less enjoyable world. Lastly, I'd like to thank my dog, Crowley. You can't read so this might be a little pointless, but you are the best critic I've ever had. Thanks for listening to me read all these lines to you at one point or another. You're a hell of a listener, and we will play fetch as soon as I finish this line.

Get yourself a group of Dirtbags and never let them go.

PREVIOUSLY PUBLISHED WORKS BY DEAD RECKONING COLLECTIVE:

FACT & MEMORY by: Tyler Carroll & Keith Dow
IN LOVE… &WAR: THE POET WARRIOR ANTHOLOGY VOL. 1
WAR… &AFTER: THE POET WARRIOR ANTHOLOGY VOL. 2
WAR{N}PIECES by: Leo Jenkins
LUCKY JOE by: Brian Kimber, Leo Jenkins, and David Rose
SOBER MAN'S THOUGHTS by: William Bolyard
KARMIC PURGATORY by: Keith Dow
WAR IS A RACKET by: Smedley Butler
THE FIRST MARAUDER by: Luke Ryan
WHERE THEY MEET by: Cokie
POPPIES by: Amy Sexauer
ROCK EATER by: Mason Rodrigue
REVISION OF A MAN by: Matt Smythe
ON ASSIMILATION by: Leo Jenkins
SANGIN, THEN AND NOW by Neville Johnson
A WORD LIKE GOD by Leo Jenkins
PHANTOMS by Ben Fortier
KILLERS IN THEIR YOUTH by Nicholas Efstathiou
DOUBLE KNOT by Mac Caltrider

DEAD RECKONING COLLECTIVE is a veteran owned and operated publishing company. Our mission encourages literacy as a component of a positive lifestyle. Although DRC only publishes the written work of military veterans, the intention of closing the divide between civilians and veterans is held in the highest regard. By sharing these stories it is our hope that we can help to clarify how veterans should be viewed by the public and how veterans should view themselves.

Visit us at:

deadreckoningco.com

 @deadreckoningcollective

 @deadreckoningco

 @DRCpublishing

Follow William Bolyard

 @justbuck__

WILLIAM BOLYARD is the author of *Sober Man's Thoughts* and the founder of *Dirtbag Magazine*. He has been featured in multiple online publications and a couple anthologies he submitted to under a fake name. Bolyard is a combat veteran and amateur adventurer. He has surfed big waves off the coast of Indonesia, dog sledded into the Arctic Circle and climbed multiple mountains across the United States. Africa is the only place he truly loves, but he currently lives in West Virginia with his dog Aleister Crowley.

www.ingramcontent.com/pod-product-compliance
Lightning Source LLC
Chambersburg PA
CBHW071155160426
43196CB00011B/2087